Praise for

"In the church and society we face unprecedented challenges. We could bury our heads in the sand or scream 'the sky is falling.' Or we could follow the lead of Sine and Friesen, who invite us to face uncertain times with courage and creativity. With relentless optimism, this book sounds the alarm and casts a vision for practical action. Let's reimagine a better future together."
—**Mark and Lisa Scandrette**, co-authors of *Belonging and Becoming* and *FREE: Spending Your Time and Money on What Matters Most*

"In a time of disorienting, rapid change and unprecedented worldwide events, the church needs trusted guides and teachers. In *2020s Foresight: Three Vital Practices for Thriving in a Decade of Accelerating Change*, Tom Sine and Dwight Friesen demonstrate that they are just the guides and teachers we need. Offering a combination of reflective wisdom, hopeful anticipation, and humble experimentation they not only help us see the future but teach us how to participate with God in creating it. Chock full of examples that challenge and inspire, now more than ever, we need books like this to give us the wisdom and courage we need for facing what feels like a daunting future. I highly recommend it and will be rereading it myself often."
—**Tod Bolsinger**, Fuller Seminary and author of *Canoeing the Mountains: Leading in Uncharted Territory*

"2020s *Foresight* has arrived just in the nick of time. It begins with a question that made me laugh out loud: 'Have you ever been blindsided by change?' The new decade has begun with a period of such unprecedented turbulence. Never in recent memory have we more needed the skills Tom Sine and Dwight Friesen write about here. In a time of continuous, accelerated change, this book is timely, practical, and inspiring."

—**Michael Frost**, Morling College, Sydney, Australia

"In 2020s *Foresight: Three Vital Practices for Thriving in a Decade of Accelerating Change*, Tom Sine and Dwight Friesen have given timely and courageous voice to their passion for the church to be a vital change leader in community. Tom has been a partner for years in encouraging scenario forecasting for Christian organizations. Dwight is a passionate advocate for churches engaging their parish. Together they have provided a timely and critical guide for church leaders to lead creatively in these challenging times, which include the economic impact of COVID-19."

—**Andrew Ryskamp**, executive co-director (emeritus), World Renew

"If there is one thing we know for sure, it's that tomorrow will not look like today. We are living in a period of incredible change, and this book will help you and your church prepare for that. In 2020s *Foresight*, get ready to have your imagination stretched and your vision enlarged."

—**Ruth Valerio**, global advocacy and influencing director, Tearfund

"I've been listening, learning, and conspiring with Tom and Dwight for a couple of decades now. I read everything they write. And this book is a lovely theological cocktail of the best of both. It's been said that the ancient prophets were not fortune-tellers but truth-tellers. They were not just trying to predict the future . . . but they were trying to change the future, by naming the present. In that Spirit, Sine and Friesen invite us to reimagine the world, and to begin building the kind of future that God wants for us and for the world. Dig in . . . and join the revolution."

—**Shane Claiborne**, author, activist, and co-founder of Red Letter Christians

"Christian leaders, if you want to dance your way through the 2020s, my friends and teachers Tom Sine and Dwight Friesen can teach you the steps you need. Intelligent, practical, and very readable. Highly recommended!"

—**Brian D. McLaren**, author of *Faith After Doubt*

"You may have thought only hindsight is 2020, but think again. Tom Sine and Dwight Friesen have gifted us with a clearly articulated vision for navigating the 'turbulent '20s.' In their new work, *2020s Foresight*, your perspective and life practices for dealing with change will increase tremendously. Today, change occurs seemingly at the speed of light. Jam-packed with explicit examples and rich references, this book and the deep wisdom contained therein, is long overdue. The thoughtful questions at the end of each chapter provide excellent group and classroom study. Do yourself and your community some good; study this book well. Sine and Friesen's timing couldn't be better!"

—**Randy Woodley**, author, earth-activist, farmer, Eloheh Indigenous Center for Earth Justice

"Tom Sine and Dwight Friesen have penned a future-facing book that is a neat blend of reflecting on the changes going on around us, practical wisdom on how to think about and respond to those mixed with imagination about what the possibilities and opportunities might be as communities of disciples seek to move from anxiety to innovation. It is interspersed with inspiring examples, questions for discussion, and even a group process outline in the middle. This is exactly the sort of conversation the Church needs to be having right now. I especially like that its focus is dreaming of a better world rather than simply being focused on the Church's internal agenda. It both stares down reality and is hopeful at the same time."

—**Jonny Baker**, director of mission education, Church Mission Society

"Sine and Friesen's 2020s *Foresight* is the book we need exactly when we need it. This book guides churches in practical ways of how to pivot and adjust well to the inevitable, and sometimes overwhelming, changes ahead. It calls the Church to be imaginative and creative, joining waves of collaboration with others on the journey. They stress being open to God's innovation in the midst of unknowns. The end result is that we will minister with hope, without fear."

—**Jamie D. Aten**, founder and executive director, Humanitarian Disaster Institute; author of *A Walking Disaster*

"2020s *Foresight* is what you get when you bring a pastor and a futurist together—namely, a theologically informed, highly practical book that helps the church prepare for a believable vision of the future. And by 'prepare,' I do not simply mean to survive, but to thrive in its mission in the world. Using the metaphor of a dance between anticipa-

tion, reflection, and innovation, Sine and Friesen lead the people of the Jesus Way to meet the challenges of our ever-changing world with prophetic grace."
—**Al Tizon**, associate professor of missional and global leadership, North Park Theological Seminary

"How do we engage inevitable change as we trust God's guidance for an uncharted future? How do we become change makers and community weavers, and how do we be the church for the world we all hope for? Tom Sine and Dwight Friesen offer time-tested wisdom, grounded stories, and accessible practices to engage these questions wholeheartedly. What an important read for this day and age!"
—**Christiana Rice**, co-director of Parish Collective; co-author of *To Alter Your World: Partnering with God to Rebirth our Communities*

"As pastor of a congregation of mostly twenty- to forty-year-olds, this book serves as both a helpful mirror of the struggles many of our members are living out in real time and a crystal ball of what lies just over the horizon. Leaders of all types will find this text immediately useful with its real-lived examples, animating questions, and respectful listening to our newest generations."
—**Ivar Hillesland**, pastor, Church of the Apostles, Seattle, Washington

2020S FORESIGHT

2020s FORESIGHT

Three Vital Practices for Thriving in a Decade of Accelerating Change

Tom Sine and Dwight J. Friesen

FORTRESS PRESS
MINNEAPOLIS

Contents

Preface

Having been co-conspirators, co-teachers, co-facilitators, and friends, it seems only right to follow our friendship into writing together. The two of us first met in the mid-1990s shortly after Dwight moved to the Seattle region. Tom had heard rumors that there was a young church planter who was trying to listen deeply to his new context while experimenting with innovative expressions, approaches to community, worship, and whole-life formation. One of my (Tom's) own life commitments has been to search out young, innovative followers of the Jesus Way to learn from them and to encourage them. So I reached out to Dwight, and we've been friends ever since.

While we are both white males, we are also very different, born of different generations and in different countries. Dwight was raised with deep roots in the Christian Anabaptist tradition on the prairies of Canada, while Tom came to faith in Jesus the Christ later in life, having spent his formative years in San Francisco. Dwight is a parish pastor and practical theologian, Tom a historian and futurist; yet together we spur one another on to discover and live even more faithfully present in the Jesus Way within the everyday stuff of ordinary life while looking with resurrection hope to the reality of accelerating changes in our culture and faith communities. We are profoundly grateful for the gift of each other.

Thank you for joining us in this vital forecasting dance. It is our prayer that you and your group will find encouragement and be emboldened to look into the future with hope as an outcome of attending to this book. The two of us love Christ and the people of God, and it is the desire of our hearts to serve both. If there has ever been an era in which you and your group of local Jesus Way followers were needed, this is it. This is your time, your era.

We would love to hear about the things you find useful in this book and how it may be having an impact on how you are planning and implementing innovation change. You can share comments with us at *twsine@gmail.com*.

1

Three Vital Dance Steps: Welcome to the Dance of Anticipation, Reflection, and Innovation in a Decade of Accelerating Change

Blindsided by Change

Have you been blindsided by change? Surprised by the unexpected? Are you among the growing number of those experiencing that "being two-weeks-behind feeling"? Commentators tell us it isn't our imagination. We are all indeed racing into the 2020s—a new decade of accelerating change . . . ready or not!

This decade of accelerating change is one of opportunity for a new generation of church leaders, Christian educators, and nonprofit executives. It is an opportunity to enable you, and those you work with, to learn how to both anticipate and creatively respond to some of these new challenges in ways that reflect the ways of Jesus. In this book, we will show you practical ways to anticipate these incoming waves of change so you can ride these waves instead of being hammered by them.

This book is written for Christian leaders who are looking for new resources and new ideas on how to not only guide their churches and Christian organizations in this decade of accelerating change, but also enable those they work with in their congregations and neighborhoods to create innovative ways to live and make a difference in times like these.

It is essential to stress that this book is also written for all educational leaders who are looking for resources to enable Gen Next to launch their lives in this much more daunting decade. These leaders include educators in our colleges, seminaries, campus ministries, and, of course, parents looking for resources. It is also written for a new generation of leaders, many of whom are compassionate, creative, and future-oriented.

Many Christian leaders have recently referred to Tod Bolsinger's book, *Canoeing the Mountains: Christian Leadership in Uncharted Territory*, as extremely helpful for leaders who are increasingly discovering that "canoeing the mountains" in these rapidly changing times simply isn't working very well.[1] Leaders in many of our faith communities, whether they are doing formation with our young, empowering families, caring for our growing number of seniors, or seeking to make a difference in our increasingly divided communities and neighborhoods, feel like they cannot

---

1. Tod Bolsinger, *Canoeing the Mountains: Christian Leadership in Uncharted Territory* (Downers Grove, IL: InterVarsity Press, 2015).

keep up with the demands of the work and the pace of the changes they experience.

As we have been doing field research with pastors, denominational executives, and new generations of leaders, we find people looking for resources to navigate this new decade of accelerated change. One pastor told us, "I think I have been planning like it will always be the '90s. I am certainly tired of being surprised and seeing those in my congregation being surprised by change that none of us expected. I want to learn to anticipate some of these incoming waves, so both my people and I have lead time to create new ways to live, empower our young, and make a real difference in the lives of our neighbors."

An Age of Acceleration . . . Ready or Not!

Tom and his wife, Christine, spent several weeks just before Christmas in 2019 visiting her family in Australia. While we were there, the most horrific firestorms in the history of Australia started spreading across the entire country. As Tom writes in early January 2020, it is clear these are the worst fires in Australia's history. "The fires have killed at least 20 people, torched more than 14.8 million acres, and 900 homes since September."[2]

And they are not done yet. Two of Christine's friends were evacuated from a town destroyed by the fires. We are no longer simply facing "climate change," we are facing a climate crisis. In fact, the 2020s could easily be the make-or-break decade in confronting this climate crisis. For the past two years, as Dwight and Tom have worked on this

---

2. Umair Irfan, "Australia's Hellish Heat Wave and Wildfires Explained," Vox, January 3, 2020, https://tinyurl.com/u89s77l.

book, we have been increasingly alarmed by the ferocity of fires in Canada and California.

"When the landmark report by the UN Intergovernmental Panel on Climate Change (IPCC) came out in 2018, there was widespread media coverage of the headline that we have 12 years to avert climate catastrophe. Where does the '12 years' come from? This is based on the number of years we have left until the carbon budget is used up for 1.5C of warming—the level needed to save most of the world's coral reefs."[3]

As you may know, seventeen-year-old climate activist Greta Thunberg has motivated millions of young people all over the planet to become activists for climate action because they want to have a viable world to live in. What you may not have heard about is that recently in the United States a new group of young people have launched Young Evangelicals for Climate Action. They not only want to influence climate policy, they want to influence Christians of all backgrounds to join them in creating a sustainable future for the planet.

In this book, we will take you on tour of a number of these accelerating challenges, including the environmental problems likely to face all of us in the 2020s and beyond. We will show you how Christian leaders can join those working locally to promote innovative actions, from rain gardens to recycling initiatives.

As concerning as the growing climate crisis is, we have recently discovered in early 2020 that we are facing a new global virus that is likely to be worse than the SARS epidemic. This new coronavirus that started in China has rapidly become a global threat to countries all over the

---

3. Dr. Helena Wright, "Do We Really Have 12 Years to Save the Planet?" Medium Environment, July 19, 2019, https://tinyurl.com/wb9xllo.

planet. It is also resulting in a shutdown and slowdown in industries all over China that serve factories and consumers worldwide. At the time of this writing in March 2020, "Italy's government has placed more than 16 million people—a quarter of the population—under lockdown in a drastic bid to prevent the spread of coronavirus."[4] Increasingly, COVID-19 is spreading to nations all over the planet, which will have a growing negative impact on the global economy.

2020's Surprise: Coronavirus Goes Global and the Economy Goes Chaotic

The major alert we announce in 2020s *Foresight* is that we are no longer simply living in ordinary changing times. Suddenly, we find ourselves living in a decade of accelerating change. However, just as we were completing this book, we were surprised by a tidal wave of this accelerating change called the coronavirus pandemic. This enormous wave is impacting lives of people all over this troubled planet.

At the point of publication, here are the huge new challenges we are facing. On March 30, 2020, the *Washington Post* reports that the United States "could record 100,000 to 200,000 deaths and millions of infections."[5]

"In Europe, Spain and Italy still face death tolls in the hundreds despite lockdowns. Australia has told people not

---

4. "Coronavirus Updates Live: Millions Quarantined in Italy as D.C. Reports First Case," NBC News blog, March 8, 2020, https://tinyurl.com/wly4zoq.

5. Brittany Shammas, Kim Bellware, Miriam Berger, et al., "New York Surpasses 1,000 Deaths in Coronavirus Pandemic as Trump Says Social Distancing Guidelines Will Remain through April," *Washington Post*, March 29, 2020.

to go outside in groups of more than two as the infection proliferates in every corner of the world."[6]

Those in Syrian refugee camps in Turkey and urban communities throughout the African continent are particularly at risk because of the density of their communities and the extremely limited healthcare resources. Denominations, Christian nonprofits, and congregations need to launch a healthcare campaign under the leadership of Christians in those countries.

Pope Francis offered "his homily against the dramatic backdrop of an empty St. Peter's Square, glistening in the rain. 'We find ourselves afraid and lost . . . We were caught off guard by the unexpected turbulent storm. We have realized that we are on the same boat, all of us fragile and disoriented . . . all of us called to row together, each of us in need of comforting the other.'"[7]

We have already been blogging on creative ways churches are "rowing together," such as people in our churches shopping for seniors and offering child care for parents who are still employed. Check out parishcollective.org and newchangemakers.com.

"The deadly pandemic is steamrolling the economies of the US and Europe as central banks and governments sweep into action to help lay the ground for a recovery from an almost-certain global recession. In the US, a record number of individuals are filing for jobless benefits while consumer pessimism increases."[8]

---

6. Avi Selk, "Coronavirus Updates," email newsletter from *Washington Post*, March 29, 2020.

7. Sylvia Poggioli, "Pope Francis Delivers Special Prayer for End to Coronavirus Pandemic," NPR, March 27, 2020.

8. Vince Golle and Zoe Schneeweiss, "Charting the Economy: Health Crisis Turns to Global Recession," Bloomberg, March 27, 2020, https://tinyurl.com/wsye6sh.

In chapter 2, we outline ways that church leaders, and those they work with, can immediately start preparing for a recession that is likely to be more daunting than the 2008–2009 recession. For example, members of Gen Z are already expressing concern that they may have an even more difficult time launching their careers and lives than millennials did during the last recession.

People all over our troubled planet are going to be dramatically impacted by this global coronavirus pandemic and global recession. It is urgent that all of us who are followers of Jesus create a rich spectrum of ways to reach out to our neighbors locally and globally and to Gen Next.

Webinars on Pandemic and Recession Prep

We will be offering webinars (see below) for church leaders, educators, and those they work with to create innovative ways to respond in your church, the lives of people in your congregation, and your neighborhood.

(1) Pandemic Prep Webinar for Life and Community Changemaking

(2) Recession Prep Webinar for Life and Community Changemaking

Church Leaders Are Already Changing

Church leaders everywhere are already switching to online and Facebook services. Thankfully, a growing number are reaching out to seniors and other vulnerable neighbors. However, much more is needed. Follow some examples of compassionate action on parishcollective.org and new-changemakers.com.

Christian Leaders Frame Guidelines
for Churches Encountering COVID-19

A number of churches are altering worship by removing the wine and only offering bread at communion, and in passing of the peace by replacing the handshake with an elbow bump. Saint Andrews Episcopal Church in Seattle, for example, has encouraged members over the age of sixty to consider staying home until the threat level subsides. A growing number of evangelical churches are exploring streaming their services online. One place to confront these twin challenges is for Christian leaders to draft some guidelines. Even more important is the need for churches to develop essential practices in serving both their congregation and the larger community. There are a number of resources for churches on how to deal with COVID-19. One of the best we have found at their website, www.brethren.org.

It Is Essential That Every Church Create
a Ministry Preparedness Plan

As we have seen, the coronavirus epidemic in China and other countries is very disruptive, resulting in the closures of schools and the shuttering of businesses. One place to begin is to create a Preparedness Committee that includes not only clergy but also leaders with medical and business backgrounds.

It is essential that church leaders focus on the needs of the elderly and low-income families in both their congregation and neighborhoods who will be hit the hardest because many of them do not have health insurance. It is estimated that there are "27.9 million uninsured and 44 million underinsured people in the US. Nonprofit health care foundation the Commonwealth Fund defines 'underinsured' as adults whose health care deductible equals 5% or more of their income, or whose out-of-pocket costs over the past year were 10% or more of their income (or 5% or more if they earned under 200% of the poverty line). By contrast, in the UK, which at the time of writing has 19 COVID-19 cases, healthcare is free at the point of delivery, meaning that people tend to see a doctor when they need one."[9]

Drawing on a range of plans recommended for church leaders in these daunting times, here is one that focuses on the needs of not only those in your congregation, but also in your neighborhood, who are not always included. Start by securing the most recent medical data from the public health organizations in your community that can inform your team about the current level of threat that the coronavirus poses. Also, contact the CDC for the most recent governmental information.[10] Use all of this information, as well as your own research of the challenges likely to face both members and neighbors, to enable your team to design your plan. Medical and financial assistance may also be available through your local government and Christian nonprofits in your community.

Learn from other congregations and communities about new ways to enable individuals and families to prepare for the impact of the coronavirus. As a part of the plan, create supplemental steps to deal with unexpected disruptions as well as community resources that might be available for emergencies. It might be essential for your team to create a

9.   Alison Griswold, "The Cost of American Health Care Could Help Coronavirus Spread in the US," Quartz, February 28, 2020, https://tinyurl.com/uhqdh25.

10. "How to Protect Yourself & Others," Centers for Disease Control and Prevention, accessed April 10, 2020, https://tinyurl.com/tbp2mxl.

supply of food and household and medical supplies to serve the needs of members and neighbors. Most importantly, it is important to create a personal care team of clergy and laity, including members with medical training, to work more personally with those in the congregation and community.

You and your team might also consider creating a website to keep both members and neighbors informed about what is happening and how they can not only pray, but also be a resource to one another. It is important in times of sustained crisis, like many communities are experiencing, to take time to celebrate every step forward. Celebrate every recovery and restored family.

Brian Walsh, an editor for *Time* magazine, recently released a provocative book called *End Times: A Brief Guide to the End of the World—Asteroids, Super Volcanoes, Rogue Robots, and More*. And no, this is not a book about the "end times." Walsh's book takes the reader on a sometimes-overwhelming journey through some of the most dire challenges that await us in the 2020s and the 2030s. Walsh's chapter on the possible threats that artificial intelligence poses for our lives is particularly alarming. However, while Walsh has written a very arresting book, he offers readers few suggestions on how our communities can prepare for and engage many of these daunting new challenges in the future. Unfortunately, there seem to be few books by Christian authors that provide creative ideas on how we can engage some of these potential crises.

Christian Leaders Preparing to Engage
a Decade of Accelerating Change

In this book, we will not only introduce Christian leaders to some local, national, and global challenges on the horizon, but will also share examples of imaginative ways that leaders, congregations, and Christian organizations are creating innovative ways to engage these new challenges. We will also share examples of how church leaders, Christian college educators, and campus ministry leaders (in groups like IVCF) are enabling those they work with to begin creating imaginative responses to some of tomorrow's challenges that clearly reflect the way of Jesus.

This book is designed to be a study resource for colleges, seminaries, campus ministries, church leaders, and study groups. It is intended to serve as a resource in churches that want to empower their members to explore and engage in innovative ways of responding to rapidly changing times in their lives, neighborhoods, and congregations that reflect the way of Jesus.

We have included questions at the end of each chapter to help individuals and groups use this as a study book. We also hope to hear how leaders and those they work with in congregations or neighborhoods are responding innovatively to these turbulent times. We are particularly interested in how those in Generations Y and Z are finding new ways to be a difference and make a difference. That is why we would also like to hear about the innovative new possibilities you and your group have created. We will post some of your innovative ideas on Tom's website, www.newchangemakers.com. We look forward to learning about your innovative responses to these turbulent 2020s.

Racing into the Turbulent 2020s . . .
Ready or Not!

Thomas Friedman, a forward-looking author and columnist for the *New York Times*, has said that "recent advances in the speed and scope of digitization, connectivity, big data, and artificial intelligence are now taking us 'deep' into places and powers that we have never experienced before—and governments have never had to regulate before."[11]

Friedman makes a compelling case that we are no longer simply living in a changing world, but are suddenly living in a world of "accelerating change." Friedman made his case while addressing an audience of British leaders on April 11, 2019, in an Intelligence Squared forum. He asked his audience the same question he had asked earlier in his last book on the subject: "What in the hell happened in 2007?"

He answered: "The iPhone happened. Big Data happened, Twitter happened, Amazon produced Kindle, and Facebook moved off campus."[12] A remarkable amount of tech change happened in less than a *decade*. As you know, in the 2020s, we are just beginning to identify not only the opportunities but also a host of new challenges that we weren't aware of when all these new tech innovations were being introduced.

Friedman skillfully responded to questions from his British audience about everything from the future of US presidential elections to the future of Brexit in the UK.

---

11. Thomas Friedman, "Warning! Everything Is Going Deep," *New York Times*, January 30, 2019, A25.

12. Thomas Friedman, Intelligence Squared forum, April 11, 2019, https://tiny url.com/wb5egbl.

However, his focus was crystal clear. All humans on planet earth desperately need to wake up to the new reality of living in a world of accelerating change.

Human beings have, of course, always lived in changing times. The reality of change is nothing new. Life is dynamic. Everything is always evolving. What is different, as we race into the 2020s, is that the rate of change happening in nearly every sector of human experience seems to be accelerating. What's alarmingly new is the accelerating rate of change that is surprising even leading forecasters. In chapter 2, we will take you on a rapid trip through a long list of daunting challenges and opportunities that we are likely to encounter in the near future.

We will start our rapid journey by giving you a quick taste of how some leaders and those they work with can start learning not only how to anticipate these incoming waves of change but also begin to find imaginative new ways to respond.

Anticipating New Opportunities for Innovative Response in Grand Rapids

Tom has been doing foresight consulting with pastors, denominational executives, and leaders of nonprofits for over three decades. He will share some examples of churches and Christian organizations that have found it very helpful to anticipate the incoming waves of change before they fully break on the beaches of the lives of those in their churches and neighborhoods.

For example, Steve Timmermans, the Executive Director of the Christian Reformed Church, recently invited Tom to do a Futures/Innovation workshop with fifty leaders of

Christian nonprofits in Grand Rapids, Michigan. Tom did advanced research on selected topics for this important session. He learned that these nonprofit leaders were doing some excellent work in a number of areas, including low-income housing. During this Futures/Innovation workshop, Tom and others they discussed some innovative ways to respond to the challenges they were facing.

Before Tom left for the workshop, he researched the future of the housing market in Grand Rapids in the 2020s, and he came across some disturbing news: two investment firms, both based in Chicago, had targeted Grand Rapids as one of the most desirable places to live in the United States. Both firms started buying a large number of homes in the area, and reportedly, these investment firms planned to hold these properties until their market values grew.

These nonprofit leaders immediately raised concerns about the impact that dramatic increases in home prices would likely have throughout their community. They immediately identified how the rising costs of real estate in Grand Rapids might force those on marginal incomes and a number of elderly couples to move out of the community, because higher home prices could trigger increasing costs for rental properties there. One leader also observed that it would also make it harder for students graduating from Calvin College to rent or buy homes in Grand Rapids.

Tom encouraged these leaders to start researching the growing number of churches likely to close in the next decade. He recommended that they join the small number of church leaders around the US who are already research-ing best practices on innovative ways to repurpose church properties as housing options for those on the margins.

Anticipating New Opportunities in Global Change-Making

Tom has found a few significant Christian organizations over the years that have incorporated forecasting as a part of their planning process. For example, Habitat for Humanity always does forecasting before they do strategic planning. They forecast where the best sites are to construct low-income housing by determining where they are most likely to find the best real estate prices. This, of course, is just smart business practice.

More recently, Tom discovered that World Vision also does some important forecasting. World Vision has long been concerned about the growing impact of the climate crisis, particularly on small-scale farmers. They do forecasting that leads to agricultural innovation. For example, one forecast of global warming in Latin America led them to work with scientists to create new forms of vegetable seed that can flourish in the increasingly warmer climates those regions are likely to experience in the 2020s.

Join Those Doing the Three-Step Dance

As we race into this new decade of accelerating change, we want to invite Christian leaders, and those you work with, to join us, and a growing community, in learning a new three-step dance:

1. **Anticipating**
2. **Reflecting**
3. **Innovating**

As you will see, we are actually inviting you to try a new way to do strategic planning in your church, Christian non-profit, or with any group that is working for change in your neighborhoods.

Step 1: Anticipating

We invite you to start your strategic planning by **anticipating** how new issues are likely to face those you work with in the next five to ten years. We encourage you to anticipate how the context is likely to change in the coming decade, not only for those you serve, but also for your church or organization. Take a cue from business innovators, urban planners, and environmental designers, who use the step of **anticipating** to identify new challenges and opportunities before they start planning. It is essential that leaders in churches, nonprofits, and neighborhood organizations also learn to anticipate new challenges and opportunities before they start setting goals.

The business sector knows that if they can anticipate what might be coming their way, then the crisis becomes their opportunity, what Harvard Kennedy School professor Ronald Heifetz refers to as the practice of "adaptive leadership." In the next chapter, we will show you how to do probability forecasting so you can enable those you work with to identify which waves are likely to come your way in the next few years. Then you can actually help them start setting goals to address that incoming wave before the waves of change fully arrive.

Learning to do forecasting before setting goals is critical for successful innovation. We recommend that you take a look at Daniel Burrus's book on business innovators, *The Anticipatory Organization*, as a starting point. Burrus too argues that we need to prepare for a decade of accelerating change. Writing primarily for business leaders, he insists, "We are living in an era of accelerating disruption—not mere change, but game-changing, transformational change."[13] Burrus explains:

> **Anticipating** needs allows organizations and individuals a means of identifying issues and problems before they occur. Not only does this eliminate the nightmare of having to react after the fact to many problems, but it also promotes the development of innovative products and services that address the needs.[14]

For example, Christian leaders are already discovering that people in their organizations and neighborhoods find themselves and their youth dealing with new technology and social challenges that didn't exist even a decade ago.

Step 2: Reflecting

Reflecting on the aspirations and biblical values of your faith is also an important part of this dance. Many faith leaders tell us that too often they assume that their theological or ethical values will automatically permeate their group's planning. However, we need to recognize that it can be very easy to lose track of the powerful undercurrent of popular culture and market forces subtly shaping even our "Christian" planning. Deep reflection is vital in a time where tech culture and targeted advertising are deeply affecting the values of all, including Christian leaders and

---

13. Daniel Burrus, *The Anticipatory Organization: Turning Disruption and Change into Opportunity and Advantage* (Austin, TX: Greenleaf Book Group Press, 2017), 10.

14. Burrus, *The Anticipatory Organization*, 10.

especially our young. This wave of technology and advertising can flood our lives, causing us to embrace aspirations and values that often contradict our core faith values.

In *The Practice of Prophetic Imagination,*[15] Walter Brueggemann reflects on the story of Israel and then the coming of Jesus to remind readers that we are called to give our lives to a different vision of a future than the one that economic globalism offers. Brueggemann's invitation is based on scripture's call to embrace an alternative vision birthed from a shalomic imagination that is devoted to difference-making instead of making a life of acquisition.

In *Mustard Seed Versus McWorld*, Tom wrote,

> We are entering an astonishing new world in which we will benefit from many of the aspects of globalization. . . . My issue is not with the architects of the McWorld future and their well-intended efforts to improve the human condition or even to make a profit doing it. . . . My problem is that, like the Babylon of old, they are making a conscious effort for all of us to redefine what is ultimate, and to ratchet up our appetites for more.[16]

What do we most value?

Step 3: Innovating

Business leaders, tech innovators, and urban planners not only lead with foresight, they also spend a lot of time and resources broadly researching best practices in their respective fields—before they start planning! As a conse-

---

15. Walter Brueggemann, *The Practice of Prophetic Imagination: Preaching an Emancipating Word* (Minneapolis: Fortress Press, 2012).

16. Tom Sine, *Mustard Seed Versus McWorld: Reinventing Life and Faith for the Future* (Grand Rapids, MI: Baker, 1999), 164–65.

quence of their research, they are able to harvest a broad range of innovative ideas from all over the planet. When they see a major new challenge racing toward them, they already have a reservoir of innovative responses to draw on. When researching best practices, a Silicon Valley company can learn from a bakery in another part of the world. A mom-and-pop jewelry store can learn best practices from Apple.

Take the realm of urban planning and new city design, for example. One of the major new cities of the future is being constructed in Toronto, Canada. You can be sure that the architects designing this City for the Future have already researched best practices from a huge range of innovative urban designs. This research includes everything from vertical gardens growing up the sides of skyscrapers in Singapore to elevated transportation systems in South America.

Global Christian organizations like Tear Fund England and World Relief often look over the fence to identify best practices in other organizations. Fresh Expressions and other leading church-planting organizations are aggressively researching best practices in this important field of innovation. However, Tom found very little research being done by church leaders looking over the wall into the most **innovative** practices in other denominations.

We urge Christian leaders, particularly those teaching a new generation of Christian leaders in our seminaries and universities, to research a broad range of best practices in their field of innovation before planning. We guarantee it will dramatically increase the quality of response, just as it does for urban planners and tech innovators.

Given the accelerating rate of change we face, it will be essential for Christian schools and seminaries, in the coming years, to place more emphasis on preparing leaders who learn not only to anticipate new opportunities but also how to research innovative practices in their field of leadership.

Innovative Practices: Creating a "Journey to Mosaic"

In his book *Future Faith*, Wesley Granberg-Michaelson provides an important forecast for all denominational leaders: the future of the church in the United States is intercultural. Gen Z will be the most racially diverse generation in America's history. Several of the leading church-planting organizations are already addressing this important trend. In fact, over the last several years, over 50 percent of all church plants in the US have been multicultural.[17]

Tom shares one remarkable denominational innovation from the very beginning of this millennium—the welcoming of a richly multiracial America. The Evangelical Covenant Church launched this particular innovation. Since I find that very few denominations research other denominations, I have become an "evangelist" sharing a "Journey to Mosaic" model with leaders in other denominations.

Leaders acted on their own growing concern for racial justice in the Covenant Church, a historically white denomination from a Swedish background. The First Covenant Church of Minneapolis was the first to start an effort to become a richly interracial church. Reportedly, it didn't take them long to create a warm and welcoming interracial

---

17.   Wesley Granberg-Michaelson, *Future Faith: Ten Challenges Reshaping Christianity in the 21st Century* (Minneapolis: Fortress Press, 2017), 24.

congregation, one that courageously began to listen deeply to their neighbors and attend to racial justice rooted in their own context. As the church community fostered a growing sense of intercultural competence, the church began to reflect the racial makeup of its neighborhood.

Then the Evangelical Covenant Church executives launched a strategy to design and pioneer new churches as a way to enable the denomination to become increasingly multicultural. They created the serious church-planting goal of making half of all their new church plants multicultural congregations. Today, not only First Covenant Church but the entire Evangelical Covenant denomination has become richly multiracial. In order to prepare their leaders to be part of a more multiracial church in a more multiracial America, they created a training program called Journey to Mosaic.

The Covenant Church invited their leaders from a broad range of racial and cultural backgrounds to get to know one another and work together with openness and mutual care by means of two very unusual bus trips. One of these Journey to Mosaic bus trips traced the Civil Rights Trail, while the other traveled the west coast, beginning in the San Francisco Bay area and concluding in Southern California. The west coast trail is a two-week bus journey that begins in an African American Pentecostal Church in Oakland, California. On the first day, participants gathered with families in that church community, sharing food and fellowship and hearing the stories and struggles of their hosts. When the leaders boarded the bus, they were intentionally seated next to someone from a different race or culture. They were then invited to process what they had just experienced with an emphasis on listening with openness and wonder. Along the journey, leaders got to spend a day in the San Joaquin Valley with migrant farm workers who shared stories of the day-to-day challenges they often experience.

Eventually, the leaders boarded the bus again and headed into Los Angeles. There, they spent time with a number of homeless families from different racial backgrounds living outdoors, in vehicles, and in other makeshift forms of housing. After each encounter, passengers would get back into the bus to process and discuss both what they had learned and how it influenced their values as leaders in the Covenant Church.

Journey to Mosaic became a meaningful and innovative way for Christians to process and prepare as followers of Jesus, together as the family of God, as they race into an increasingly interracial future.

Wouldn't it be a good idea if seminaries and Christian colleges that offer courses in leadership training had graduate students do broad research on a wide range of innovative practices like Journey to Mosaic? These graduate schools could then share this growing list of innovative practices with church leaders to expand their range of responses to the new challenges of the 2020s.

Witnessing Surprising Innovation in Britain in 2016

In early November 2016, Dwight invited Tom to lead a workshop at the New Parish Conference in Birmingham, England. It was the first time we had worked together, and Tom welcomed the opportunity. Tom led a workshop called "New Generation Creating New Social Enterprises in

Britain." Since he was already in the UK speaking on the future of urban innovation, it worked out smoothly.

In preparation for his time in the UK, Tom read a number of articles on the recent referendum in Britain in which a slim majority of voters had leaned toward Brexit, a proposal to exit from the European Union. Tom found the legislation very complex and divisive. The articles indicated that Britain's departure from the EU would likely be very long and uncertain.

After the plane landed in London on the morning of November 8, 2016, Tom headed for baggage claim. Suddenly, he heard a voice over the speaker system announcing the outcome of an another very divisive vote back home in the United States. Donald Trump had been elected president. Tom found himself wondering how Christians in both Britain and the United States would respond to these two divisive elections.

Several weeks later, after Tom completed his address on the future of urban innovation at the New Wine event, he headed to Birmingham to meet me (Dwight) in an Anglican cathedral. We took a quick tour and then listened to an engaging plenary by Paul Sparks, one of Dwight's two compatriots in the New Parish Movement. Paul received a warm response from a younger audience of over 200 participants.

Immediately after the plenary, Tom led a workshop for young innovators in the UK who were creating new social enterprises. These included a start-up bakery in London that trained unemployed young people to become successful bakers. Tom also attended the last workshops of the New Parish Conference, titled "The Brexit Exit" and hosted by Mike Royal, an Afro-Caribbean Pentecostal bishop who was working as a consultant for a broad range of mission groups in the UK. The forty men and women in attendance were mostly pastors or lay leaders in their churches, most of them living in Birmingham, a city that has more low-income residents than any other city in Britain.

As everyone settled in, Mike had us all introduce ourselves. Tom was immediately impressed by how skilled a facilitator Mike seemed to be, but he had no idea of what to expect of the workshop. Mike started the session in a surprising way. He simply asked people, in small groups of three, how they felt about the recent Brexit vote. Responses were somewhat slow at first. Then people started to share very candidly how they felt about this very divisive vote. As people on both sides of the Brexit divide shared their opinions, the energy in the room picked up.

As Mike brought that exchange to a conclusion, the room was about evenly divided between those who favored Brexit and those who opposed it. Mike then invited this divided group to spend a few moments discussing whether Brexit was likely to have a long-term impact on Britain in the coming decade. Again, this divided group amazingly reached remarkable consensus. Both groups predicted that Brexit would likely be a long-term issue for leaders in the UK. They also predicted it would likely have a major negative impact on the British economy. Which, of course, would have a negative impact on the people and churches in Birmingham that existed on marginal incomes.

Mike shifted the workshop quickly from the likely impact of Brexit on their neighborhoods in Birmingham to how God was calling church leaders through scripture to respond to these new challenges. Some of the women leaders were first to respond. They stated that clearly, as followers of Jesus, we are called to not only love God but our neighbors in Birmingham as well. Clearly, even though this group was divided on their view of Brexit, they reached a clear consensus on their responsibility, as followers of Jesus, for the community in which they lived.

Mike masterfully shifted the conversation again, asking participants to work in small groups and to come up with ways they could, as followers of Jesus, address the coming cutbacks that were likely to impact their neighbors. The sense of division that had been in the room just twenty minutes earlier completely disappeared. Participants worked in small groups to come up with plans to start community gardens in vacant lots and on church properties. Others suggested that a group of churches start hosting rummage sales now so that they would have resources to help their most vulnerable neighbors when the cutbacks came. It was remarkable to witness a group of people who were so divided politically become so united in a common cause out of genuine concern for their neighbors. In spite of their clear political divide, these followers of Jesus left that conference committed to implementing new ways of working with their neighbors to help them make it through what was likely to be very tough season for people all over the UK.

Doing the Three-Step in Birmingham

Looking back on this New Parish Conference in 2017, it was easily the most memorable workshop Tom had experienced in recent years. This was due largely to the skillful leadership of Mike Royal. It occurred to Tom that Mike was leading in a process very much like the three-step dance we are proposing in this book:

Step One: Mike helped workshop participants *anticipate* how their neighbors would likely be impacted by the coming economic cutbacks.

Step Two: Mike enabled these neighbors who were divided politically to *reflect* on their biblical responsibility to their most vulnerable neighbors.

Step Three: Mike enabled the leaders to use a creative process to *innovate* new ways for their churches to help empower neighbors before the cutbacks came.

This three-step dance in Birmingham could impact communities all over Britain facing cutbacks in the early 2020s.

Now let's fast forward to 2020. Boris Johnson has been elected as the new Prime Minister of the UK, and he plans to push Brexit through in one year. However, "Boris Johnson's own official government figures show Brexit will make British people much poorer."[18]

No sooner had President Trump been acquitted of impeachment by the US Senate on February 5, 2020, than the Democrats made a stumbling beginning in the presidential race in Iowa. The outcome of this election will not only have an impact on the American people, but people all over our planet in this time of accelerating change.

Racing into the Turbulent 2020s

It seems that society has become even more divided since we were at the New Parish Conference in 2016. In the next chapter, we will take you on a quick tour of some the new

---

18.   Adam Bienkov, "Boris Johnson's Own Official Government Figures Shows Brexit Will Make British People Much Poorer," January 17, 2020, https://tinyurl.com/y6ot3la8.

opportunities and challenges we are likely to encounter as we continue to race into the turbulent 2020s and creative ways we can engage them in the Three-Step Dance. We will show those in leadership, and those they work with, not only how to anticipate the incoming waves but also how to form innovative responses to the waves that reflect the way of Jesus.

However, we want to conclude this chapter by celebrating the advent of Christ, which reminds us that the God of all hope has not forgotten God's people or our troubled world as we race into the turbulent 2020s.

Welcoming the Good News of Advent as We Race into the Turbulent 2020s

"'It's nothing less than a manifesto for turning the world upside down," Jim Wallis declares in *Sojourners*. "In Advent, our thoughts turn to the meaning of Christ's coming and the deep significance for the followers of Jesus—'waiting for him to come, which has special and poignant meaning for us in the deep political and moral crisis in which we find ourselves.'"[19] In many ways, Advent is Tom's favorite liturgical season, because it invites Christians to do the work of preparing our hearts for what it means that God came and lived as one of us in a world that needed—and needs—to be changed.

Jesus's birth is an event destined to culminate in his sacrifice for our personal atonement and reconciliation, but it also radically transforms the earth with the kingdom of God. From the beginning, God's promise of good news to

---

19.   Jim Wallis, "It's Nothing Less Than a Manifesto for Turning the World Upside Down," *Sojourners*, 2019.

the poor and liberation for the oppressed characterized the incarnation. "He has brought down the powerful from their thrones and lifted up the lowly; he has filled the hungry with good things, and sent the rich away empty,"[20] said Mary, the mother of Jesus, who seemed to understand the meaning of his coming. This is the Jesus who began his public ministry by quoting the prophet Isaiah, saying, "The Spirit of the Lord is upon me, because he has anointed me to bring good news to the poor. He has sent me to proclaim release to the captives and recovery of sight to the blind and let the oppressed go free, to proclaim the year of the Lord's favor."[21] This is "nothing less than a manifesto for turning the world upside down."[22]

Prayer

Creator God,

When we are honest with ourselves, we have to admit that the amount of change coming our way can be overwhelming. Yet, we know that you have not given us a spirit of fear. You invite us—even dare us—to live lives marked by resurrection hope. What do we have to fear? While aspects of tomorrow may feel unsettling, you invite us to join you in the remaking of all creation. Teach us to read the signs of the times. Guide us to discern what is ours to do. Embolden us to innovate in accordance with your shalomic imagination. Amen.

---

20.   Luke 1:52–53.

21.   Luke 4:18–19.

22.   Wallis, "It's Nothing Less Than a Manifesto."

For Group Discussion

1. What is your initial reaction to the topics introduced in this chapter? What additional time and information do you need to anticipate new challenges and research innovative responses?

2. What are some specific resources you might explore to help you anticipate some of the new challenges or opportunities in your own life and those you work with in your congregation and local community as we race into this decade of turbulent change?

3. What are some resources you might have students check out to enable them to discover innovative responses they might adopt to respond to these new waves of challenge and opportunity?

4. Which of these new innovative responses to the incoming waves of opportunity reflect the ways of Jesus?

5. How could incorporating the three-step dance of **anticipating**, **reflecting**, and **innovating** change how you plan as a leader?

6. Which of the new challenges we are likely to face in the 2020s cause you the greatest concern for the future of your loved ones, those you work with, your church, or your neighborhood?

7. Select one or two of those new challenges you identified, then Google them to find two or three other imaginative, new responses to those incoming waves of change, and be ready to share them with others in the class.

8. Identify which of your responses you have come up with that most fully seem to reflect the aspirations and values of the Jesus we seek to follow. Be ready to share your **Anticipations**, **Reflections**, and **Innovations** in your class at the next meeting.

Resources

Tod Bolsinger, *Canoeing the Mountains: Christian Leadership in Uncharted Territory* (Downers Grove, IL: InterVarsity Press, 2015).

David R. Brubaker, Everett Brubaker, Carolyn Yoder, and Teresa J. Haase, *When the Center Does Not Hold: Leading in an Age of Polarization* (Minneapolis: Fortress Press, 2019).

Wesley Granberg-Michaelson, *Future Faith: Ten Challenges Reshaping Christianity in the 21st Century* (Minneapolis: Fortress Press, 2017).

Rita McGrath, *Seeing Around Corners: How to Spot Inflection Points in Business Before They Happen* (Boston: Houghton Mifflin Harcourt, 2019).

Willie James Jennings, *The Christian Imagination* (New Haven: Yale University Press, 2011).

2

Anticipating New Opportunities in the Turbulent 2020s

Knowledge is telling the past. Wisdom is predicting the future.
—W. Timothy Garvey

Join Those Catching Waves Instead of Being Hammered by Them

Tom will never forget, one beautiful Maui morning, as a huge wave came racing toward shore. It was his second day of learning to surf and his first day trying to catch a wave. He dug into the surf with both hands. It was 1968, and he had accepted a position as the Dean of Students at Maui Community College. Two weeks after arriving, he borrowed a huge old nine-foot surfboard from a friend and started heading to the beach on the weekends. Here is what he learned.

Sitting on his board in the water twenty-five yards from shore, he suddenly saw a promising wave heading his way. It arrived sooner and with much more force than he expected. It sent the heavy nine-foot board careening into the air. Tom instinctively dove as deep as he could to avoid the painful calamity of being hammered by his plummeting board.

After four weeks of surfing like this, he finally learned the valuable lesson that most surfers learn. He figured out how to anticipate the waves that would give him a great ride and avoid those that could cause him great peril. Most importantly, when he caught the wave, he learned to jump from his stomach to his feet in one swift motion.

We love the title of Tod Bolsinger's book *Canoeing the Mountains*. Picture the imagery of Lewis and Clark canoeing west and then suddenly being confronted by the Rocky Mountains. Imagine how daunting the unexpected mountain ranges must have been for them . . . and they never saw it coming. As Bolsinger observes with great foresight, "The world in front of you is nothing like the world behind you."[1] It is way beyond even the largest waves surfers confront.

Anticipating the World in Front of You

We are, however, experiencing much more daunting challenges globally and locally than Lewis and Clark ever experienced. We encourage leaders to try and view these incoming waves of change in the 2020s as new opportunities—for us and those we work with. They provide the

---

1. Bolsinger, *Canoeing the Mountains*.

opportunity to locate or create innovative responses that reflect the aspirations of Jesus.

In this chapter, we will take you on a trip back to the future. We will then survey some of the escalating waves of change that are likely, in this decade, to crash on the beaches of our lives, families, communities, and congregations. Then we will briefly explore some of the growing global and national challenges, many of which will also require imaginative new responses.

In chapter 1, we introduced you to the three-step dance that helps you anticipate and creatively respond to these new opportunities in the turbulent 2020s while reflecting the way of Jesus. In this chapter, we will show you how to anticipate and creatively respond to the incoming waves of change. Those of us who are leaders in our churches, Christian nonprofits, universities, seminaries, and campus ministries can no longer serve those we work with as though the future will simply be an extension of the past. We have entered a time of accelerating change. As a consequence, we need to join those who learn to **anticipate** the new challenges and opportunities so they have lead time to form **innovative** responses that **reflect** something of the way of Jesus.

We encourage Christian leaders to join business innovators, urban planners, and environmental innovators to consider changing how they do planning to be more effective leaders in a time of accelerating change.

We encourage leaders in Christian organizations, in these rapidly changing times, to learn to start with two important forms of research before setting any goals or drafting a single strategy. We urge you (1) to anticipate new challenges that you and your organization are likely to face in the coming decade, so you have lead time to respond;

and (2) to broadly research best practices, like a business innovator or urban planner, so those you work with have a broad range of strategies to draw from as you seek to engage those new challenges.

Learning to **anticipate** change will give you important lead time to search for the most innovative response. We also encourage you to prioritize **reflecting** on the values of Jesus as you imagine your responses. Finally, in step 3, we will select new innovative responses that both engage the new challenges and reflect the way of Jesus. For some, this may mean exploring innovative programs in other denominations. For others, it means identifying creative solutions being tried in the larger society. The goal is enabling those we work with to enact **innovative** responses that effectively engage these incoming waves of change.

Anticipating New Opportunities with Probability Forecasting

We are constantly impressed by how many leaders in other fields begin their planning process by forecasting first. The reason that so many business leaders devote so much time to this first step is that it has such high payoff. Spending time **anticipating** new challenges gives them lead time to form new responses and avoid treacherous disruptions. Business innovators use a range of sometimes complex methods of forecasting. For our purposes here, the most useful form of forecasting for church leaders is "probability forecasting."

Daniel Burrus, author of *The Anticipatory Organization*, stated in Forbes that, "If we continue to solve problems after they happen, we'll only struggle to keep up with more and more disruptions as they come." The future may feel unknowable, but Burrus assures us that "we can nonetheless create pretty accurate predictions. . . . When we do, it gives us more certainty in an uncertain world. It changes how we plan and innovate."[2]

Burrus goes on to explain that leaders need to decide between "hard trends and soft trends."[3] We will describe the hard trends he calls as "probability forecasting." These trends offer solid evidence of where disruption is likely. Soft trends tend to have weaker evidence to support them. Obviously, when leaders identify a soft trend or uncertain forecast, they need to be more cautious. In this chapter, we will attempt to focus on the more probable, and thus actionable, forecasts.

For example, a researcher could make a highly probable forecast on how many people now in their fifties in the US will retire in 2030 and likely be very accurate. However, if the same researcher predicted how the US economy will perform twelve months from now, it would be hard to have confidence in his forecast due to its being based on very soft trend data.

Business leaders and urban planners use a broad range of other forecasting strategies to enable them to anticipate new challenges and opportunities. One example is scenario forecasting, a process by which you draft three alternative future scenarios ten years ahead. Leaders essentially test their strategic plans through each scenario to determine if their plans will be able to engage the different possible

---

2. Ron Carucci, "Beyond Agility: How Your Future Is More Certain When You Know How to Anticipate It," *Forbes*, June 26, 2016, https://tinyurl.com/rn732mq.

3. Daniel Burrus, *The Anticipatory Organization: Turning Disruption and Change into Opportunity and Advantage* (Austin, TX: Greenleaf Book Group Press, 2017), 21.

futures. Tom has used this process effectively with organizations like World Relief and World Concern.

Another method, called the Delphi Process, is used by businesses to harvest a cross-section of informed options about what changes could take place in the future. Essentially, the Delphi Process involves giving multiple rounds of questionnaires to a selected panel of experts on a given issue. After the participants respond to these repeated rounds, their responses are aggregated to provide leaders with an expert opinion on given trends in the future.

However, for church leaders, we are going to exclusively focus on the kind of probability forecasting that Daniel Burrus recommends, since it is the most straightforward way for Christian leaders to anticipate possible changes facing those in their congregations, their neighborhoods, and in their international work.

Many Christian leaders today are surprised by change much more than they should be. A critical reason is that leaders in churches are seldom trained on how to forecast before they plan. Numbers of leaders report how unanticipated change can drastically undermine even their best plans as well as the lives of those they work with.

Futures Innovation Workshops for the Turbulent 2020s

One of the kinds of probability forecasting we recommend to leaders in a congregation before they lead them in a Futures Innovation Workshop is to research how their neighborhood context is likely to change in the next five to ten years. A Baptist church in San Bernardino had a thriving youth program with seven full-time staff. A realtor in the church researched the local housing market and discovered that real estate costs were likely to accelerate so quickly in the next five years that most young families with kids were not going be able to afford to live there. This research led leaders in the church to start planning how to reach out to an aging population while recognizing that their youth programs were bound to decline.

A Presbyterian congregation discovered the benefits of forecasting how their neighborhood was likely to change. In fact, they created some innovative new programs for their new neighbors that would not have occurred to them if they hadn't done some research on how their neighborhood was changing.

When Tom worked with this Presbyterian church in Los Angeles, he asked them to do some research before he came. In addition to doing some probability forecasting regarding attendance and giving patterns, he also asked church leaders to have a local realtor research how real estate in their neighborhood was likely to change. And this congregation made a very different discovery than the Baptist church we just discussed.

The realtor discovered, with some surprise, that developers had overbuilt several blocks of low-income apartments near the church. As a consequence of reduced rental prices, the apartments were beginning to attract a number of single-parent families. So, during the Futures Innovation Workshop, one creativity group focused on creating a way to respond to this new opportunity.

They divided into two innovative teams. The first designed a new hospitality program to welcome these new neighbors with information about the neighborhood and all of its resources. Since they learned that a number of their new neighbors were struggling with issues of childcare and sustainable employment, the second team of lay leaders designed new programs to help address the needs of this new population that was just beginning to arrive. This program included offering classes on everything from parenting to classes on job hunting.

By developing the vital practice of **anticipating** change and enabling people to form **innovative** responses, churches, nonprofits, colleges, and groups like the New Parish are inventing new ways to do community empowerment with their neighbors in ways that reflect the hospitality of Jesus. This will become increasingly important with the growing number of aging congregations in the 2020s.

As Tom consulted with Tear Fund leaders in London, he discovered they were doing a very thorough job of anticipating the changing needs of the poor families they worked with in small communities in Africa and Asia. However, they had not been tracking the data on how their donor base was likely to change in the coming decade.

They gave Tom access to their donor data, and he showed them the bad news: they were likely to face a serious decline in giving in the next two decades. The age profile of their faithful donors showed that the donors were aging more rapidly than they had realized. The median age of givers was fifty-five, and they had very few supporters in their twenties and thirties.

Tom invited the leaders to come up with a response to address this new challenge. And the Tear Fund staff responded, creating a new process called Art for Mercy, which was designed to reach twenty- and thirty-year-olds in churches they worked with. They hired a successful young church planter to head this new venture.

Over the next year, they invited twenty- and thirty-year-olds in churches all over Britain to create original art about

Tear Fund's work in a range of different countries. They presented their work in publications and presentations. It not only helped promote the important work of Tear Fund, but also engaged a younger generation of supporters in ways that enabled them to use their skills in reflecting God's love for neighbors struggling with their own disruptive waves of change half a world away.

Anticipating New Incoming Waves in the Turbulent 2020s: Ready or Not!

We want to offer church leaders a quick profile of some of the incoming waves of challenges and opportunities we are likely to face in both your churches and your neighborhoods in the 2020s and beyond. We encourage leaders to consider sharing some of these important trends with those they work with. We would also encourage those people to start researching innovative ways to engage these incoming waves in a timely fashion. As you read down the list, we suspect many leaders will identify those in your congregation or neighborhood that are likely to be most impacted.

We have researched and compiled some challenges and opportunities that we are likely to face in this new decade that deserve our attention and, where possible, our creative response. We start this tour by considering some of the new challenges facing our youth, our seniors, and those at the margins. We will also briefly tour some problems likely to face Western societies, not the least of which is another possible recession in the 2020s. Finally, we will share some ways to start preparing for these incoming waves now.

We will finish this section with a brief look at the future

of the church globally, but particularly in the West. We offer a very modest sketch of some possible new global changes and challenges as well. We hope that some of these forecasts will be helpful in facilitating new forms of innovative response that reflect the biblical call for compassionate advocacy of justice for our neighbors, globally and locally.

This engagement is also guided by our three-step dance:

1. **Anticipating** the likely impact of some of the incoming waves;

2. **Reflecting** on your biblically informed response; and

3. **Identifying innovative responses** based on your research and study of best practices. We encourage you to launch those innovative responses prayerfully and take care to monitor the impact of your responses with those you work with.

Anticipating the Challenges and Opportunities Awaiting Gen Next

One of the most important areas of anticipatory research for Christian leaders is to profile each new generation for the purpose of getting a sense of challenges and opportunities that await them in every decade. Too often, in the past, some of us have assumed that each new generation is simply a carbon copy of the last generation.

Thankfully, in recent decades, many older adults have started reading the research profiles of each new generation from a Pew Research study[4] and a range of other

---

4.   Where Millennials End and Generation Z Begins, www.pewresearch.org, 2019.

research centers. This research is essential reading for parents, educators, and youth workers to encourage the gifts of and engage the new challenges facing each new generation.

Gen Y, also known as millennials, were born between 1981 and 1996 and are 56 million strong in the US, surpassing the Boomer generation. Members of Gen Z were born 1997 to 2012 and are 65 million strong, making them the largest and most multicultural generation in the United States. We would encourage parents and Christian leaders in Canada, the UK, and Australia to research the characteristics of Gen Y and Z and the challenges they are likely to face in their countries as well.

We will start by identifying some of the new changes that Gen Y and Z are already encountering, as well as some of the new challenges and opportunities they are likely to face in the 2020s and beyond. We will also identify some of the good news that both of these generations could bring to all of our lives, churches, and societies.

Anticipating New Waves of Opportunity for Gen Y and Z in the Turbulent 2020s

We have shared the vocational satisfaction of working with and learning from younger generations of seminary students who are still educating and enlightening us.

Millennials (Gen Y): The Delayed Generation

A number of the first wave of millennials, who launched their working lives during the 2007–2009 recession, are still trying to catch up. This recession made it harder for millennials to find jobs, go to college, and launch their lives. Reportedly, many have also postponed getting married, starting families, and buying homes. Student loan debt for many Americans grew at a worrisome and unprecedented 102 percent. Millennials are facing $1 trillion in student loan debt, according to Bloomberg.[5]

In Britain, home ownership has also plummeted among millennials, not only in London, but throughout the UK. It has dropped by more than half in some regions of the country. As a consequence, many millennials have longer commutes to work, and more are living in shared housing. Many from this generation, in the US, the UK, and other countries, are reportedly finding it harder to secure work and find housing. Adding to this is the fact that their combined school loan and credit card debt fully qualifies them to be described as the "Delayed Generation."

Most church leaders in North America and Britain are aware of the bad news from Pew Research that millennials are a leading group among "the nones and the dones." They are the first generation in which many are choosing no longer to affiliate with churches. Slowly, evangelical pastors are discovering that putting on a hip show and wearing skinny jeans isn't working anymore.

Church leaders also need to learn that many millennials that do choose to affiliate will not be as generous as Gen Xers and Boomers, because many of them are already facing more economic challenges than older generations. Even though a higher percentage of Gen Z will attend college, Gen Z is likely to be saddled with a higher level of college debt than any prior generation, which will make

---

5. Alexandre Tanzi, "Millennials Are Facing $1 Trillion in Debt," Bloomberg, February 25, 2019, https://tinyurl.com/y47dr3vc.

it much harder to launch than it was for their parents' or grandparents' generations.

Gen Z: The Post-Millennial Generation

Some church leaders have discovered that both Gen Y and Z are the good news generations. For example, it is reported that some Silicon Valley firms are actually adding a social mission to their corporate policies to motivate these compassionate and creative young millennials to work for them.[6]

Gen Z is America's most multiracial generation. When looking at the numbers for nonwhite people in each generation, Gen Z has 48 percent, compared to 39 percent in Gen Y (Millennials) and 30 percent in Gen X. Also, a higher percentage of Gen Z are going to college than prior generations.

Furthermore, "Gen Z has never known a world without smartphones and social media, so it's even more engrained for them than millennials. They gobble up information quickly and are ready to move onto the next thing in an eye blink."[7] Reportedly, Gen Z is also less active sexually. Also, like Gen Y, they tend to be more accepting of gay and lesbian relationships than older generations.

However, since Gen Z is so media connected, they seem to be more media vulnerable. They are particularly affected by critical remarks made by acquaintances on social media. Also, Pew Research reports, "seven in ten US teens see anxiety and depression among their peers."[8] According to the

---

6. Tom Sine, "Live Like You Give a Damn!," *Plough Quarterly*, 2016.

7. Ryan Scott, "Get Ready for Generation Z," *Forbes*, November 28, 2016, https://tinyurl.com/s8u8env.

8. Juliana Menasce Horowitz and Nikki Graff, "Most U.S. Teens See Anxiety

American Psychological Association, "this generation is 27 percent more likely than other generations, including millennials (15 percent) and Gen Zers (13 percent) to report their mental health as 'fair to poor.'"[9]

Clearly, parents, educators, and church leaders need to be sure that those in Gen Z are given the kind of support they need to deal with everything from online abuse to other serious emotional issues as they seek to launch their lives in challenging times like these.

Those who comprise Gen Z are also more apprehensive of confronting a dangerous shooting situation in their school or other public places than prior generations. Not surprisingly, they also tend to favor more rigorous funding for gun control policies, as do many in Gen Y.

Reportedly, Gen Z students prefer to participate in volunteer activities that are likely to bring long-term change rather than simply volunteering at a food bank:[10] "Roughly defined as those currently aged seven to twenty-two, we're nearing the age when we can make a significant impact on the world. Some of us—like the school shooting survivors who created March for Our Lives—already have."[11] They also seem to be managing their economic resources more effectively than either millennials or Xers.[12]

What is most important to convey about Gen Z is that they are more gender inclusive and they care deeply about

and Depression as a Major Problem Among Their Peers," February 20, 2019, https://tinyurl.com/y39mgh6x.

9. Sophie Bethune, "Gen Z more likely to report mental health concerns," *American Psychological Association* 50, no. 1 (January 2019).

10. William Gale, Hilary Gelfond, and Jason Fichtner, "How Will Retirement Savings Change by 2050? Prospects for the Millennial Generation," The Brookings Economic Studies, March 2019, https://tinyurl.com/rmx2gbx.

11. Michael Pankowski, "Gen Z Will Change the World," October 7, 2019, https://tinyurl.com/yylwws5e.

12. See HSastore.com, "Gen Z Is Leading the Way with Savings Habits."

issues of racial, economic, and environmental justice. We urge church leaders to invite both their ideas for empowering forms of social enterprise and justice advocacy for times like these.

Gen Y and Z: Facing a Very Uncertain Economic Future

Tom is surprised when many parents, educators, pastors, and youth workers don't seem to be aware that many in Gen Y and Z raised in the middle class may not be able to retain the economic lifestyle they experienced as youth. Those who are supporters of these generations can learn much from business leaders about how to do basic economic forecasting to identify economic challenges that both Gen Y and Z are likely to continue encountering. For example, one of the major new economic realities is that 45 million borrowers have a total student debt that exceeds $1.5 trillion. Each quarter, student debt increases by $30 billion at interest rates as high as 13 percent. Over the past decade, student debt has more than doubled.[13]

This will likely mean that growing numbers of those in Gen Y and Z will have to postpone getting married, starting families, buying a home, and making enough to save for a secure retirement. As a consequence, a number in these two generations will likely also have to postpone retiring unless they receive more help now in dealing with educational and credit card debt in order to successfully launch.

---

13. Harry Dent, "Millennials Are Not Buying Homes Like Boomers Did," Economy & Markets, February 28, 2019, https://tinyurl.com/wrpej4l.

Gen Y and Z: Delaying Homeownership

The Brookings Institute states, "Compared to previous generations, Millennials are more likely to delay homeownership, marriage, and child-bearing. Young adults currently have the lowest home ownership of any similarly aged generation since at least 1989."[14]

"Missing Millennial Homeownership Endangers the American Dream" is the title of an article written by Andrea Riquier. She points to a report from the Urban Institute's Housing Finance Policy Center that suggests the story of millennials and homeownership is, in many ways, a story of inequality in America and one that is getting worse. "Boomers bought real estate at unprecedented speed and price, thereby inflating a housing bubble from 1983 into 2005. Demand drove up prices. And that made them richer, especially the ones born earlier."[15]

However, there is growing evidence that millennials are already having much more difficulty purchasing homes than the Boomer generation did. First, costs in a growing number of markets have escalated much more quickly than salaries. Add to that their debt burden, and it makes it difficult to qualify for loans for even inexpensive homes. It is not likely that many in Gen Z will have an easier time purchasing homes than Gen Y. And home ownership could become even more challenging for an increasingly multiracial generation unless we can see all housing discrimination policies removed.

In our conversation on **Reflection** in chapter 4, we will

---

14. Harry Dent, "Millennials Are Not Buying Homes Like Boomers Did," Economy and Markets, February 28, 2019, https://tinyurl.com/sqk4tzy.

15. Andrea Riquier, "Missing Millennial Homeownership Endangers the American Dream," MarketWatch, July 12, 2018, https://tinyurl.com/wtn3dfr.

directly explore if the aspirations and values of the American Dream are compatible with the aspirations and values of the way of Jesus. We will invite readers to do some new dreaming that can open the door to imagining not only alternative ways of living, but even the designing of new forms of dwelling, not only for Gen Y and Z, but for other generations as well as for life in the turbulent 2020s and beyond. As you will see as we continue to identify incoming change, we will all need much stronger social networks in our living arrangements, neighborhoods, and congregations to enable us to deal with all kinds of incoming waves of turbulence and trouble.

Gen Y and Z: Facing an Even More Uncertain Retirement Future

Tom's good friend Dan, who happens to be Gen Y, helps schoolteachers develop plans to start saving and investing to prepare for retirement. Dan reports, not surprisingly, that the hardest teachers to convince they need a retirement program are those under forty. Teachers who are older than fifty are more receptive to financial planning. For the reasons listed above, the Brookings Institute predicts that millennials are likely to save too little for their retirement.[16]

Serious questions are being raised about whether social security and other federal programs for seniors will still be available in the US when both Gen Y and Z reach their senior years. The reason for this concern is that the size of the federal deficit could become so large by then that those important programs will no longer receive adequate fund-

---

16. Riquier, "Missing Millennial Homeownership."

ing. "The future of any society, by definition, depends on its ability to boost the health and well-being of the next generation. When we devote the resources necessary to support families and improve the services and programs that help all children be healthy, get a good education, and contribute to our nation's future success, we all benefit. Instead, we are shortchanging and failing our children. The *Washington Post's* Catherine Rampell refers to the current situation as a 'War on Children' and the *Post's* Petula Dvorak writes how, on issue after issue, the country is 'failing its children.'"[17]

All Gens Facing a Very Uncertain Retirement Future

The research below reveals that many Americans, like many in other countries, have not made adequate provision for retirement, particularly those that work for a modest wage and are able to place very little into savings. The research shows that a definite ethnic bias is an influence in the marketplace.

For example, "Whites are more likely than other groups to have a retirement account. As of 2016, 65.9 percent of whites have a retirement account, compared to 37.8 percent of blacks and 34.1 percent of Hispanics."[18] The Brookings researchers, who are attempting to predict retirement savings patterns until 2050, describe it as "an exercise in uncertainty. There is clearly a cause for concern. First, many members of the current generation of retirees and near-retirees are not saving very much. Second, Millennials

---

17.   Bruce Lesley, "Shortchanging Our Children Harms the Nation," September 16, 2019, https://tinyurl.com/r3ogzqs.

18.   "How Will Retirement Savings Change by 2050?," www.brookings.edu, 16.

will face a number of 'headwinds' in accumulating enough savings to finance adequate retirement. Third, the projected rise in the minority population will reduce retirement savings adequacy, if current trends persist."[19]

An article on the future of humanity projects a concern for those in the US who will be retiring between now and 2030. They report, as Vanguard states, "fewer than half of all Americans age fifty-five to sixty-four have at least $70,000 in their retirement accounts. Another survey in 2016 by Go Banking Rates found only 26 percent had retirement savings greater than $200,000, while 60 percent had less than $50,000."[20]

The Atlantic states that middle-class Americans are increasingly experiencing "The Great Affordability Crisis"; inequality is growing for the middle class and the next generation. Even though a high percentage of Americans are working at the onset of the 2020s, the cost of housing, healthcare, student loan debt, and childcare are rising more rapidly than people's income. This is accelerating the rate of inequality in America and is placing growing pressure on the middle class and making life almost impossible for those with low incomes.[21]

The implications for the next two decades is that "The Great Affordability Gap" means many from Gens Y and Z are struggling with much higher school debt than earlier generations; because of that, they are postponing having children and will likely have many fewer children.

This could lead to the United States becoming a graying

---

19. Riquier, "Missing Millennial Homeownership," 14.

20. Scott Lanman and Katia Dmitrieva, "These Are the Signs a US Recession May be Coming," Bloomberg, February 13, 2019, https://tinyurl.com/vf7lqtt.

21. Annie Lowrey, "The Great Affordability Crisis Breaking America," *The Atlantic*, February 7, 2020, https://tinyurl.com/yx7d4uda.

society like Japan and most of Europe. That would mean fewer people to run our factories, go to our stores, and pay taxes. That would mean higher demand for healthcare by people over fifty, which would likely drive up prices for everyone, which could result in the possibility that social security will not be available for today's youth when they retire.

We are heading into a future of not only accelerating change but also increasing disruptions, from weather-related disasters and health disruptions like the coronavirus to growing economic pressures on those at the margins in many of our communities. We invite clergy and lay leaders in our churches to organize a lay group like the Parish Collective (https://www.facebook.com/parishcollective/) in order to enable their neighbors to deal with these disruptions in ways that empower them. This includes preparing for the next recession.

Coronavirus Spreads Recession Fears Around the World

"As odds of a global recession rise, governments and central banks around the world are racing to fend off the economic damage from the spread of the coronavirus."[22]

Is it a great deal to ask both clergy and lay leaders who are in the early stages of preparing for the coronavirus, which is invading our communities, to also begin preparing for a possible economic recession in the turbulent 2020s?

Some readers will remember the natural disaster when

---

22. Jim Zarroli, "Coronavirus Spreads Recession Fears Around the World," NPR, March 5, 2020.

Katrina devastated New Orleans in 2005. That disaster motivated denominations all over the United States to create a range of disaster response teams and strategies. Some denominations, such as the ELCA, already had a disaster response team in place. However, for others, such as the Southern Baptists, it was a wake-up call. They now maintain a remarkable disaster feeding program. For example, the Southern Baptist Church recently responded to a tornado in the Midwest by dispatching a portable kitchen to the site to feed hundreds of people. Ever since Katrina, major denominations like the United Methodists, the Mennonites, and the Presbyterians have natural disaster response capabilities.

When it comes to the next recession, most major corporations have strategic responses in place. They are equipped to navigate through another recession. However, there are currently few denominations or local churches that have created any recession preparedness strategies.

A few of us in Seattle started seeing data in 2007 that we could be headed into a major recession in the US. We organized a Recession Preparedness Innovation session with fifty Christian leaders several weeks before the incoming economic waves began to hammer the lives of people in Seattle. Several Presbyterian churches developed websites where members could post things they wanted to share with those in their congregations and their communities. This included everything from a car in their driveway to an extra room in their homes:

Trinity Lutheran Church in Lynnwood, Washington, was proactively trying to enable middle-class members to both reduce their vulnerability and increase their availability to others. They are offering a course on financial planning to help people both reduce their debt and create budgets to better steward what God has entrusted to them. They also offer a course, taught by older members, on how to grow and process food (i.e., canning fruit) to reduce food costs in tough times.

Young innovative leaders are not only creating new expressions of the church, but some are actually downscaling their lifestyles so they have more to share with the needy.[23]

More Creative Recession Responses

Here are some more creative ideas our friends came up with at our Recession Preparedness session:

Churches need to design innovative disaster plans and train crisis response teams to offer support for people in serious economic peril, helping them identify available employment and financial assistance resources.

Inventory available resources of the church community (i.e., tools to borrow, plumbing, or mechanical skills, kitchen space or utensils, financial advice, extra work clothing) and create a kind of church Craigslist (or 'Kingdom List') for trading, bartering, or borrowing.

Convene classes on financial stewardship focused on the biblical principles of reducing debt, budgeting, giving, and saving. Offer financial mentorship. Promote lifestyle changes that can save money and free up funds to help those in serious need.[24]

---

23. Tom Sine, "Are You Recession Ready?," *Leadership Journal,* January 25, 2009, https://www.christianitytoday.com/pastors/2009/winter/areyourecession-ready.html.

24. Sine, "Are You Recession Ready?"

How Families and Individuals Can Prepare for Recession Next

It is essential that all of us begin to dramatically change our financial practices to enable us and our loved ones to weather the next recession whenever it comes.

Bankrate offers seven ways to recession-proof your finances. We list the first three here, but please reference the footnote to view the other four.

1. Pay down debt

It's crucial that you pay down any outstanding debt—more specifically, high-cost debt, such as your credit card balance—to create some breathing room in your budget. Often, economic downturns lead to job loss. If you're worried about job security, paying off your obligations might bring you more peace of mind. Prioritize credit card debt, then turn to other types of loans, such as mortgages or auto loans. Student loans, however, have more favorable provisions, which makes paying them off less of an urgency, says Greg McBride, CFA, Bankrate's chief financial analyst.

2. Boost emergency savings

Job loss can also make it difficult for Americans to pay their day-to-day expenses.

Beefing up your emergency fund—that is, the pool of cash that you reserve specifically for events like downturns—can make it possible for you to still afford your necessities while you search for a new position.

Even if you're paying down debt, it's important that you prioritize saving. Focus first on loading up your emergency fund with one month's worth of living expenses. After that, pay off your debt, and then focus on building up a reserve of three to six months' worth of funds . . .

"Everyone needs to have a cash cushion, even while they're attempting to pay off high-interest rate debt," Anastasio says. "It's imperative because, if an emergency arises and you're putting every dollar toward eliminating debt, you have no choice but to go back to credit cards to cover the expense."

A high-yield savings account can help you earn more on the money you stash away. Shop around for the best account that suits your needs and lifestyle.

3. Identify ways to cut back

Before a downturn begins, it's a good idea to go through your monthly expenses. Identify which items are discretionary—services or items you don't need—and which items are a necessity. The discretionary items are most likely ones that you can either eliminate now or in the future, McBride says.

"Certainly your starting point would be the discretionary items—subscription services or even just spending patterns," McBride says. "Dinners out or nights out at the bar with friends can seriously add up over time."[25]

We also urge churches and Christian nonprofits to start putting away buffer funds to enable you and your organization to weather a serious recession and continue to share resources with neighbors near and far. We suggest learning best practices from some of our Mormon friends, who often seem to be more prepared for the next disasters than most of us. We need to prepare in ways where we can also share with our neighbors.

---

25.   Sarah Foster, "7 Ways to Help Recession-Proof Your Finances," Bankrate, August 22, 2019, https://tinyurl.com/shxbnkb.

Facing a Volatile Global Economic Future

Now, we will shift our focus from possible challenges at the national level in many of our countries to the future of the global church. Given increasing challenges we are likely to face in this troubled decade nationally and globally, we are particularly concerned not only by the graying and declining of our churches in the West, but even more by the declining levels of giving and volunteering. The need seems to be ramping up locally and around the world.

At the same time, we want also to draw your attention to the larger global economy and explore how the leadership of the global economy is likely to change. We focus especially on economic challenges likely to face our poorest neighbors, to say nothing of the looming environmental crisis and the growing number of totalitarian regimes around the world. We will seek to identify innovative ways that people of faith can make a creative difference in our turbulent tomorrows.

Facing a Tidal Wave of Tech Change: Ready or Not!

Our looming tidal wave of technological changes will include the expansive development of artificial intelligence, which could dramatically increase surveillance in our personal lives. The rapid development and deployment of robotics could produce less expensive products, but it could also have a seriously negative impact on both living-wage jobs and even some higher-paying jobs.

It seems likely that drone taxis will be a part of our future by the end of the 2020s. They are already being tested in Oregon.

A drone air taxi designed by Airbus has successfully completed 114 test flights in Pacific Northwest skies. Airbus, along with its rival Boeing and many others, is striving to make flying cars an option for your urban commute. The enthusiasm around the test flight hangar in Pendleton, Oregon, has to be leavened, though. Industry insiders said the technology is running years ahead of regulators and public acceptance.[26]

All the major tech firms seem to be increasingly struggling with ethical and political challenges as the media increasingly cause racial and political division while undermining the integrity of democratic governments. This is likely to manifest an increasing challenge to local and national governments in the 2020s. For example, "California Consumer Privacy Act Explained AB 375 will go into full effect on January 1st, 2020. . . . All fifty states have enacted legislation to protect consumers' private information, but some states have more stringent laws and penalties than others."[27]

China: Facing a New Number One Global Economy—Ready or Not!

Tom remembers the very warm spring day in the early 1980s when he traveled from urban Hong Kong to a small rural village in mainland China. It was his first and only trip to China. He couldn't have been more surprised at what he encountered that day. It was truly like falling through a time warp.

Suddenly, he found himself in a kind of rural US village

26. Tom Banse, "In the Skies of Eastern Oregon, an Autonomous Robo Taxi Takes Flight," Northwest News Network, October 10, 2019, https://tiny url.com/ubwp7ra.

27. Juliana De Groot, "What Is the California Consumer Privacy Act?," Digital Guardian, July 15, 2019, https://tinyurl.com/qmf3yfs.

in the 1920s with small shops with roofs that looked like they were collapsing. Donkeys pulling worn-out wagons exemplified a level of rural poverty that was unlike anything he had ever seen before. Tom doubted that any international leaders back then could have imagined that this largely agrarian nation would become a dominant global economic and technological power, taking a leading role in shaping our common future in the 2020s and beyond as it recovers from the impact of COVID-19.

This new high-tech China has created the most sophisticated surveillance state of any government on the planet. However, China is now using surveillance technology in hopes of ensuring rigid political conformity by their people. China is likely to become the number one surveillance society on the planet, using facial recognition technology and incentives for the general population conforming to government expectations.[28] They also have active "re-education" centers for their Muslim residents and others. The ongoing resistance currently happening in Hong Kong also seems to be heading toward a major crisis that is likely to create uncertainty not only in China but throughout Asia as well.

China is also becoming a dominant technological power, and their reach is expanding all over the planet. China is buying up ports in Europe, farmlands in Africa and Latin America. Their powers of economic and political surveillance are rapidly expanding all over the planet as well. Their new, expanding highway system is outdistancing the vast US freeway system and provides another way for them to transport goods in the region.

---

28.   Emile Dirks and Sarah Cook, "China's Surveillance State Has Tens of Millions of New Targets," Foreign Policy, October 21, 2019, https://tinyurl.com/u6yfmhj.

Facing Russia's Growing Global Political Influence

Even though Russia has a relatively small economic profile compared to China, the United States, and other developed nations, their political influence is growing in Europe as they increase their influence in former Soviet bloc nations. They have become a major and problematic force in the Middle East. All US intelligence services are warning that highly trained Russian operatives will be even more active in the 2020 elections in the United States, seeking to influence both Republican and Democratic voters, not only seeking to influence the outcome of the presidential election but to increase divisions and animosity throughout American society.[29]

Global Cyber Risk: Ready or Not

One of the major ploys that Russia, China, or Iran could direct toward the US is the recent and growing threat of cyber attack. "'A cyber attack should be expected': U.S. strike on Iranian leader sparks fears of major digital disruption," declared the *Washington Post* on January 3, 2020, after a US drone strike killed one of Iran's top generals, Major General Qassem Soleimani.[30]

According to the article, such a cyber attack could be much more disruptive than most people realize. Regardless of who launches a cyber attack on the US, it could cause

29.   Adam Goldman, Julian E. Barnes, Maggie Haberman, and Nicholas Fand, "Lawmakers Are Warned That Russia Is Meddling to Re-elect Trump," *New York Times*, February 20, 2020, https://tinyurl.com/sjtsplo.

30.   Tony Romm, Isaac Stanley-Becker, and Craig Timberg, "'A Cyber Attack Should Be Expected': U.S. Strike on Iranian Leader Sparks Fears of Major Digital Disruption," *Washington Post*, January 3, 2020.

huge chaos. It could be targeted to attack utilities all over the US, impacting millions. Or banks could be targeted, not only disrupting the nation's economic order but also compromising large amounts of personal data. The economic grid could be essentially shut down for a period of time. While a nuclear threat is always present, a cyber attack causing widespread disruptions seems to be much more likely.

Global Risk Report: Ready or Not!

The Global Risk Report 2019 was published against a backdrop of worrying geo-political and geo-economic tensions. This report is the work of a thousand decision makers from the private sector, academia, and civil society who participated in the Global Risks Perception Survey. The report warns that "[o]ver a ten-year horizon, extreme weather and climate change policy are seen as the gravest threats."[31]

Growing numbers of activists from Gen Y and Z, who are aware of the gravity of the threat to our good earth, are increasingly leading protests all over the planet. Somehow, people of faith need to join those who understand this new reality. If we don't start to reverse the enormously destructive environmental forces and their causes in the 2020s, we might lose our last opportunity to secure the creation and its climate for future generations.

In recent years, thousands of people in California, Canada, and Australia have directly experienced devastating fires that demonstrate the escalating costs of extreme weather events. Burned homes often make the evening news, but there are other stories we seldom hear about.

---

31.   Global Risks Report 2019, World Economic Forum, https://tinyurl.com/yd2o3hhl.

Our poorest global neighbors are once again facing daunting new levels of deprivation and hunger. *The Guardian* reports that "global hunger has reverted to levels last seen a decade ago, wiping out progression of improving people's access to food, and leaving one in nine people undernourished last year; the third annual rise since 2015, with most regions of Africa and of South America showing worsening signs of food shortages and malnutrition. More than a billion of the world's hungry live in Asia."[32]

Furthermore, they continue, "The reversal of progress made in slowing malnutrition in the first half of the decade has caused concern among international agencies. Climate shocks, such as droughts and floods, were identified by the UN as 'among key drivers' for the rise [of malnutrition] in 2017, along with conflict and economic slowdowns. Nearly 100 million people were left dependent on humanitarian aid during the year."[33] We live in a world of growing need and global division.

In the Global Political Polarizing 2020s: Ready or Not!

As an eight-year-old growing up in San Francisco at the end of World War II, Tom witnessed firsthand the early workings of the United Nations. He watched as black limos brought leaders from all over the world to those first planning sessions at the Fairmont Hotel located a block from the apartment where he lived with his parents. Tom said he and his parents were keenly aware of how close the United

---

32. Fiona Harvey and Karen McVeigh, "Global Hunger Levels Rising Due to Extreme Weather, UN Warns," *The Guardian*, September 18, 2018, https://tinyurl.com/w3n2u5v.

33. Harvey and McVeigh, "Global Hunger Levels Rising."

States and other nations came to being a part of a catastrophic political disaster. Even at this young age, he remembers feeling lifted by an incredible sense of hope for the future.

Later, we both watched the Berlin Wall come down and totalitarian nations become democratic nations virtually overnight. In one of Tom's earlier books, he wrote with deep gratitude, "The dance on the Berlin Wall was the dance of God, the songs sung in the streets of Soweto with the release of Nelson Mandela were the songs of God, and the prayers for the peace of Jerusalem were the prayers of God."[34]

However, one of the most alarming trends we will see in the 2020s is the rapid rise of totalitarianism again, not only in Eastern European countries, but in Western democracies as well. In the United States, we are witnessing growing racism, anti-Semitism, and increased political polarization in families and social media. We are likely to see not only Russia but other countries, such as China, benefiting from sowing division and even fabricating their own versions of reality to increase the divisions in our society. For example, *Sojourners* reports that "Putin positions himself and Russia as the defender of Christian Civilization."[35]

We encourage all churches—mainline, evangelical, and Catholic—to create new forums in all communities to help people of all backgrounds to decode and debunk the propaganda of fear, anger, and hate. Christians of all traditions have a historic opportunity to create new ways to listen to

---

34. Tom Sine, *Wild Hope* (New York: W Pub Group, 1991).

35. David Gushee, "The Trump Prophecy," *Sojourners*, May 2019, https://tinyurl.com/uvdcxbt.

one another with empathy, reject divisiveness, and work for the common good in the 2020s and beyond.

Shrinking Christian Response in the Turbulent 2020s

How will our churches be a part of a creative and compassionate response in the 2020s? The forecast is not encouraging.

We regularly gathered church attendance and membership statistics from the Presbyterian, Methodist, Episcopalian, Southern Baptist, and Mennonite churches. All show a trend downward in terms of membership and worship attendance. The past decade has shown the same pattern of decline even in the most evangelical churches. The Southern Baptists, for example, report that their congregations are graying and declining, just like mainline churches.

The new reality is that the entire church in the West is in crisis. Unless we find some new ways to engage Gen Y and Z by the end of the 2020s, we are likely to see a huge closure of churches all over North America and other Western countries. Dwight is already contacting denominational leaders in the United States to hold symposiums on repurposing church properties to provide low-income housing and other programs of empowerment for our most vulnerable neighbors while maintaining a meeting space for some shrinking congregations.

The State of Church Giving through 2016 reports that the state of church benevolence giving from 1968 to 2016 provides a revealing glimpse of the impact of the graying and declining membership in the United States. This survey reports that benevolence giving to help our poorest neigh-bors locally and globally declined during this period by a deeply disturbing 75 percent.[36]

2020s Ready or Not! We Need Ignited, Compassionate Imaginations

Wesley Granberg-Michaelson offers a powerful forecast on the future of the global church:

> Today, Christianity is undergoing another major historical shift. For the first time in more than one thousand years, a majority of the world's Christians are living in the Global South. This trend is accelerating, constituting the most dramatic geographical shift in the history of Christianity. For four hundred years, Western culture shaped by the Enlightenment has been the comfortable home for the dominant expressions of Christianity in the world. Now all that is changing. Christianity has become predominately a non-Western religion.[37]

While the global church is growing, the churches in the West are in increasing danger of disappearing. If the churches in North America are going to avoid heading down the path of churches in Western Europe, we will need the Spirit of God to ignite our imaginations. We will need to create new expressions of churches committed to serious change-making, and we will also need to create new forms of life-making where we can free up more of our lives to be present to God and our neighbors in times like these.

---

36. John L. Ronsvalle and Sylvia Ronsvalle, *The State of Church Giving through 2016: What Do Denominational Leaders Want to Do with 8 Billion More a Year?* (Champaign, IL: Empty Tomb, Inc., 2018).

37. Wesley Granberg-Michaelson, *Future Faith: Ten Challenges Reshaping Christianity in the 21st Century* (Minneapolis: Fortress Press, 2017), 1–2.

In the next chapter, we invite you to join us by **reflecting** on how scripture calls us to a more serious whole-life faith as followers of Jesus. Then, we will show you some novel ways to create new forms of community and new approaches to neighborhood change-making, and to join those creating more innovative expressions of church for times like these.

Those of us in leadership need to enable those we work with to discern what is important and what is of value in our lives, the lives of our youth, in our congregations and the communities where we live. We need to make a compelling case for who we are called to be as followers of the servant Jesus for the coming decade and beyond.

Theologian Cornel West names the power of Christian hope in the face of seemingly insurmountable oppression, in the face of what seems like it's just too much:

> Last, but not least, there is a need for audacious hope. And it's not optimism. I'm in no way an optimist. I've been black in America for 39 years. No ground for optimism here, given the progress and regress and three steps forward and four steps backward. Optimism is a notion that there's sufficient evidence that would allow us to infer that if we keep doing what we're doing, things will get better. I don't believe that. I'm a prisoner of hope, that's something else. Cutting against the grain, against the evidence. William James said it so well in that grand and masterful essay of his of 1879 called "The Sentiment of Rationality," where he talked about faith being the courage to act when doubt is warranted. And that's what I'm talking about.[38]

---

38.   Cornel West, "An Abiding Sense of History," Wesleyan University Commencement Address, May 30, 1993, https://tinyurl.com/uav99h4.

Prayer

Loving God,

When you created all that is, you called it "good," even "very good." Yet when we look at the signs of our times we can sometimes feel like things are not so good anymore. By your Spirit we ask that you help us anticipate the probable changes, not with fear, but with abiding resurrection hope. Help us look to the future as an active way of demonstrating our love of you by loving our neighbors as we love ourselves. Give us the courage we need to look realistically at these accelerating changes so we can meet them with sober judgment, shalomic imagination, and collective resolve. Remind us again and again that you are making all things new. And aid us as we spur one another on in love and good deeds. Amen.

For Group Discussion

1. What are the key advantages of **anticipating** some of the new opportunities and challenges we are likely to face in the turbulent 2020s and beyond?

2. What are some examples of probability forecasting in your own life, family, or workplace? What are some possible creative responses to the incoming waves of change?

3. What are some of the new challenges and opportunities that are likely to face Gen Next in the coming decade in terms of the costs of schooling and housing? What are some innovative ways to help Gen Next reflect something of the compassion of Jesus?

4. What are some of the local challenges that are likely to face your most vulnerable neighbors in the next ten years? What are some creative ways to become involved that might reflect some of the hospitality of Jesus?

5. What are some new challenges and opportunities facing your congregation in the next ten years, and what are some imaginative ways to respond that might reflect some of the good news of Jesus and expand your care for neighborhood empowerment?

6. How might your church start preparing for the next recession before it comes so that your people are not only ready in their own lives, but they are also ready to be there for their neighbors?

7. What are some new global challenges from those dealing with the climate crisis to increasing agricultural empowerment in more vulnerable regions? What innovative responses have you found in your research that address these accelerating changes in your life and in the lives of those with whom you work?

8. In these increasingly divided times, how could your church become a center for celebrations and mutual respect across race, class, and political divides that reflects the way of Jesus?

Resources

Chris Bradley, Martin Hirt, and Sven Smit, *Strategy Beyond the Hockey Stick: People, Probabilities, and Big Moves to Beat the Odds* (Hoboken, NJ: Wiley, 2018).

Michael K. Girlinghouse, *Embracing God's Future without Forgetting the Past: A Conversation about Loss and Nostalgia in Congregational Life* (Minneapolis: Fortress Press, 2019).

Josh Packard and Ashleigh Hope, *Church Refugees: Sociologists Reveal Why People Are DONE with Church but Not Their Faith* (Loveland, CO: Group Publishing, 2015).

Michael Tchong, *Ubertrends: How Trends and Innovation Are Transforming Our Future* (Ubercool Innovation, 2019).

Kevin Kelly, *The Inevitable: Understanding the 12 Technological Forces That Will Shape Our Future* (New York: Penguin Books, 2016).

3

Reflecting: Where Will We Find Hope in the 2020s?

A society concerned with shalom will care for the most
marginalized among them.
God has a special concern for the poor and needy,
because how we treat them reveals our hearts,
regardless of the rhetoric we employ to make ourselves sound just.
—Randy S. Woodley

Anthony Levandowski, a Silicon Valley engineer, filed papers with the US Internal Revenue Service for the Church of Artificial Intelligence, called the "Way of the Future." In the papers he filed, he explained that it was for the purpose of "the realization, acceptance, and worship of a Godhead based on Artificial Intelligence (AI) developed through computer hardware and software." Levandowski told *Wired*, "It's not a god in the sense it makes lightning and causes hurricanes . . . but if there is something that is a billion times smarter than the smartest human, what else are you going to call it?"[1]

In response to this, Thomas McMullan asked in a Medium post, "But is the technological industry exploiting this deeply embedded language? If god is a projection of a society's hopes and dreams, then are these sentiments already being hijacked by the type of techno-utopianism spouted by Facebook, Google, Amazon, etc., with or without a 501(c)(3) tax status?"

McMullan presents us with an interesting observation for our reflection: "Digital technology, AI included, has appropriated the discourse about hope . . . the hope of higher productivity, easier interactions, faster connections, better products, and more social contacts. . . . The rhetoric changes, but the fundamental promise is that a new digital technology will be better than an old one in fulfilling more promises." Then McMullan adds, "The risk is the digital techno-hope may manipulate and exploit people, replace any other kind of hope, including spiritual ones."[2]

Will We Find Hope in a Time of Tech Saturation?

Is McMullan right? Does digital technology, AI included, not only offer an endless stream of tech **innovation** but also cast a new vision of hope that replaces even traditional "spiritual ones"? In this chapter, we want to shift our attention from simply **anticipating** some of the new challenges

---

1. Thomas McMullan, "Living in the Machine, the Word of God: How AI Is Defined in the Age of Secularism," Medium, January 18, 2018, https://tinyurl.com/wsznnnr.

2. McMullan, "Living in the Machine."

we are likely to face in the 2020s in order to **reflect** on what our core aspirations and values are and where they come from.

In the last chapter, we focused largely on enabling those in leadership, in churches and Christian organizations, to focus on **anticipating** new social, environmental, and demographic changes so they and those they serve have enough time to respond.

In this chapter, we will invite you to do the three-step dance again. We will start by **anticipating** some of the growing impacts of Big Tech and particularly how it is affecting our lives and those of our youth, especially our aspirations and values.

Dancing the Three-Step in a New Big Tech World

Step 1. **Anticipate** the impact of Big Tech in our lives and those of our young people in the 2020s.

Step 2. **Reflect** on the aspirations and values of Big Tech and consumer culture. Where, in this new tech age, will we find hope and a way of being that more fully reflects the aspirations and values of Jesus and that first community?

Step 3. We will suggest **innovative** ways to live, create community, make a difference, and celebrate that more fully express our hope.

Anticipating: How Could New Tech Undermine Our Ability to Find Hope?

First, let's go back to the future. Most of us find ourselves engulfed in a rapidly growing avalanche of both new tech and Big Tech. Most of us value the evident benefits new tech has given us. However, it has come at a cost. Most of us are spending much more of our waking hours on screens than we ever expected or intended to.

Let's take a candid look at some of the downsides of this age of tech acceleration and tech innovation. Many people in your congregation and community are likely finding that their schedules in daily life are also becoming much busier. As a professional consultant, I often hear that people have less time for face-to-face contact with friends. A number have also reported that while they enjoy some online devotionals, they seem to have less time to reflect on scripture and pray for loved ones. A certain number also report that they seem to have less time for church activities.

The Atlantic reports that "ninety-five percent of Americans ages thirteen to seventeen years old have a smartphone or access to one, and nearly half report using the internet almost constantly."[3] Reportedly, many teens are now on screens six to ten hours a day. That is a huge increase for both Gen Y and Z. Reportedly, a remarkable number of young adults are even sleeping with their screens. We are learning that many are getting up multiple times during the night to text their friends or further divert their attention to video games.[4]

The Pew Research Center reported that 54 percent of the thirteen- to seventeen-year-olds surveyed spend what they deem too much time absorbed in their phones. Sixty-five percent of the parents agreed. Vicky Rideout, "who runs a research firm that studies children's interactions with media and technology, was not surprised by this finding. . . . 'They are dealing and grappling with the same chal-

---

3. Joe Pinsker, "Phones Are Changing the Texture of Family Life," *The Atlantic*, August 22, 2018, https://tinyurl.com/y8z26wct.

4. Pinsker, "Phones Are Changing the Texture of Family Life."

lenges that (adults) are, as far as, they are living in the context of a tech environment that is designed to suck as much of their time onto their devices as possible."[5]

While the time spent on our phones is rapidly growing, the exact opposite is happening in terms of participation of most church members and their youth in the United States, which we will discuss more later in this chapter. Rideout has some advice for parents: "The way parents interact with technology, then, shapes the way they interact with their kids and the way their kids interact with technology. If parents put away their phone at dinner and charge it in a different room when they sleep, it helps kids realize they too can exercise some control over the devices." She added, "Google and Amazon provide parents with software that enables them to restrict their children's access to certain apps or activities."[6]

This new technology also requires a new level of parental supervision. Pew Research reports that nearly six in ten parents check the websites their teens visit as well as look through their teen's cell phone call logs and messages they receive.[7] Shockingly, Amazon retains children's data even after parents believe it has been deleted.[8]

5. Pinsker, "Phones Are Changing the Texture of Family Life."

6. Pinsker, "Phones Are Changing the Texture of Family Life."

7. Monica Anderson, "How Parents Feel about—and Manage—Their Teens' Online Behavior and Screen Time," Pew Research Center, March 22, 2019, https://tinyurl.com/y53gn9px.

8. Josh Golin and Jeff Chester, "Advocates Demand FTC Investigation of Echo Dot Kids Edition," Center for Digital Democracy, May 9, 2019, https://tinyurl.com/rk4cdcm.

What Info Is Big Tech Collecting
from Us and Our Youth?

Let's briefly explore how the tech companies continually collect more personal data from us and our youth. Once collected, they then sell our personal information to a number of corporations. They use it to customize their ads to influence us to purchase more of their products. We are told that these ads are also designed to shape our aspirations, values, and our sense of what is important.

"It's 3 a.m.—Do you know what your iPhone is doing? Mine has been alarmingly busy. Even though the screen is off and I am snoring, apps are beaming out lots of information about me to companies I have never heard of. Your iPhone is probably doing the same—and Apple could be doing more to stop it," writes Geoffrey Fowler at the *Washington Post.*[9]

Shoshana Zuboff, in her new book *The Age of Surveillance Capitalism*, asks the question in a more compelling way: "Can the digital future ever be our home?" She answers her question this way: "The digital realm is overtaking and redefining everything familiar even before we have had time to ponder and decide."[10] A troubling indictment.

What Public Health Concerns
Are Advocates Raising?

Thankfully, while many of us seem to be asleep to this remarkable invasion of our lives, some reporters and con-

---

9. Geoffrey Fowler, "While You Are Sleeping Your iPhone Stays Busy—Snooping on You," *Washington Post*, May 28, 2019.

10. Shoshana Zuboff, *The Age of Surveillance Capitalism: The Fight for a Human Future at a New Frontier of Power* (New York: Public Affairs, 2019), 4.

sumer watchdogs are awake to and reporting on these issues. Ron Yokubaitis reports:

> Today, internet service providers, social media, and search engines develop and sell your profile. Sometimes, these marketing companies develop or buy popular apps so they can directly collect information. Your digital property is making money for everyone involved in the process—except you.
>
> The part that is disconcerting is that it is usually done without my knowledge or consent. This is especially troubling when it comes to my children's information, as kids now are more in touch with electronics than any generation before them. It is time to take our privacy back from tech companies.[11]

Golin and Chester reported, "Today, a coalition of 19 consumer and public health advocates led the Campaign for a Commercial-Free Childhood (CCFC) and the Center for Digital Democracy (CDD) called the Federal Trade Commission to investigate and sanction Amazon for infringing on children's privacy through its Amazon Echo Dot Kids Edition."[12]

An investigation by CCFC and other groups "revealed that Echo Dot Kids, a candy-colored version of Amazon's home assistant with Alexa voice technology, violates the Children's Online Privacy Protection Act (COPPA) in many ways. Amazon collects sensitive, personal information from kids, including their voice recordings and data gleaned from kids' viewing, reading, listening, and purchasing habits and retains it indefinitely."[13] In the last chap-

---

11. Ron Yokubaitis, "It's Time to Take Our Privacy Back from Tech Companies," The Hill, January 19, 2018, https://tinyurl.com/yb9ew8g7.

12. Golin and Chester, "Advocates Demand FTC Investigation."

13. Golin and Chester, "Advocates Demand FTC Investigation."

ter we documented the law passed by the State of California, which goes into effect January 2020, stating that Big Tech or corporations can no longer sell our personal information or information they have gathered about our children without our permission.

Are We Facing a Crisis of Formation?

In *Mustard Seed Versus McWorld*, published in 1999, Tom raised concerns about who will shape the values of our youth. He asked if it is possible that the church and parents could be facing "a crisis of formation" in the future. Tom wrote, "The marketers of McWorld are increasingly trying to sell meaning and identity. Consumer culture and pop media are increasingly attempting to take over the role the family and the church once held—helping young people finding a sense of purpose and identity." He added further, "the young people were spending thirty-seven and a half hours online a week,"[14] which in comparison to today seems much less significant.

There was no sense at all, in 1999, of the coming explosion of such a huge range of new tech firms or the accelerating influence they would have on us through "Instagram envy" or FOMO ("fear of missing out"). However, it is clearer today that we are indeed facing an accelerating crisis of formation. We see this crisis of formation happening for two primary reasons. First, those we work with tell us that a growing number of families are only bringing their children to worship once or twice a month instead of every week. Second, children who have their own cell phones have access to a huge range of information that reflects a

---

14.   Sine, *Mustard Seed Versus McWorld*.

broad range of values, many of which contradict the values of their faith.

Our question now is not only for parents but for pastors and religious educators: How can forty-five minutes of Sunday school two to four times a month possibly compete with the influence of six to ten hours a day online? A few parents make time to provide religious home schooling. However, for those that do, it is a drop in the bucket given all their children's onscreen time and all the propaganda that advertisers are sending their way. Plus, some current video games are making a great deal of money while instilling an attraction to gambling.

Here are the two examples of how followers of Jesus have found alternative ways to put their Christian faith first with Gen Next in this decade of accelerating tech change. Hopefully, examples like these will enable us to consider new ways to steward the screens in our lives and in the lives of our youth.

Hopeful Alternatives for Gen Next

Raising the Kids Off-Grid

This year Tom Wuest, who is a farmer from Ohio, was the lead guitar player at the Inhabit Conference sponsored by the New Parish. This high-energy conference always welcomes a very multicultural community to the Seattle School of Theology and Psychology.

Wuest and a small group of musicians had led our worship sessions at Inhabit last year. He also stayed in Tom and Christine Sine's guest room, as he had done the year before. This year Wuest asked to sleep up in our prayer tower, on the floor, instead of sleeping in a bed in our guest room. He told us that he enjoyed both the sacred profile of our small prayer room and also the stunning view of the Olympic Mountains.

Last year, we learned that Wuest and his wife Karen had made an unusual decision after they graduated from Regent College in Vancouver. They were both deeply concerned about the growing media exposure that their two preschool sons were likely to face. Out of a growing concern for their boys and for the environment, they purchased a family farm in Ohio and made the decision to live off the grid.

Their two preteen sons have grown up without smartphones or even a television. They do use some computers at school, so they know how to use technology. However, they have no interest in having their own smartphone or any of the online opportunities that go with it.

Wuest says his sons enjoy reading books, playing soccer at school, and spending a couple of hours helping their dad on the farm every day. These boys are completely happy living a largely tech-free lifestyle. This, of course, is a very rare example and beyond the reach of most parents.

Monasticism, Old and New

Gerald Sitzer is a professor at Whitworth University and an author who writes compelling books on spirituality. He has also become a very successful Christian innovator with the support of the Lily and Murdock foundations. When Tom talked to Gerald recently, he was delighted to discovered that one of Gerald's concerns is the future of Gen Y and Z in our new high-tech world. Gerald found that many of his students were distracted by too much tech in their lives, which seemed to be taking a toll on their social and spiritual lives.

So Gerald invented a month-long retreat experience for twenty-five students at a time. When they sign up for this opportunity, they have to agree to very rigorous restrictions on the use of their iPhones. In fact, they were not allowed to keep them in the room where they slept during the retreat.

The focus of the retreat was to introduce students to a range of different expressions of Christian formation. Essentially, the format was to introduce them to fashioning daily spiritual disciplines for themselves, drawing on both ancient and contemporary spiritual practices.

Gerald said that because students are largely off tech for the month, the retreat is a new time of discovery for them. They not only discover the richness of new spiritual practices, something many Gen Z youth seem to miss out on, but they experience the delight of simply spending time with one another and the satisfaction of face-to-face conversations.

Before the month ends, the students develop a plan for their spiritual disciplines when they return to Whitworth and for continued stewardship of technology in their daily lives. Gerald says this experience helps them develop more discipline in all areas of their lives. Not surprisingly, some report that they still struggle with the responsible stewardship of tech in their lives.

Invitation for Christian Leaders and All Followers of Jesus to Reflect

Dwight suggests a very good idea: consider creating groups to revisit some of our ancient Christian practices. Here are some of his suggestions for small groups of Jesus followers who are hungry for a more vital and whole faith.

Looking Backward: Reflective Practices

Fortunately, as we look back to the Mothers and Fathers of our faith, we find out how they wisely sought to navigate their times. We inherit from them rich traditions to draw from when engaging in the collective work of discernment and reflection. We offer one such reflective practice that we think is especially helpful today: *Lectio divina*.

Reflective Practice: Lectio Divina

The three vital practices of this book actually find resonance with the practice of reflective scripture reading pioneered by Saint Benedict of Nursia around the sixth century. Saint Benedict guided his community into an anticipatory Bible-reading process he called *Lectio divina*, which translates loosely as "listening for God."

It's a pretty simple process.

A small portion of scripture is read three separate times. Each reading has a slightly different listening posture, intonation, and cadence. The "listening-first" posture is simply asking, "What captures your attention?"

Then, hearers are invited to listen to the same Bible reading through the lens of what had captured their attention on the prior reading: "What do you think God might be saying to you?"

Finally, hearers are invited to listen to the same Bible reading through the lenses of the first two hearings, this time wondering: "What might God be inviting you to do or become?" Benedict described this whole process as listening with the "ears of your heart."

Lectio divina is a beautiful way of thinking about the forecasting work we are inviting you and your group to engage in. Christian forecasting might be understood as a spiritual practice of listening for the voice of God through probable changes within your cultural context.

Lectio divina's first hearing invites the openness of **anticipating**. Its second hearing invites the discernment of **reflecting**. And its third hearing invites the kind of shalomic action birthed from the third practice, **innovating**.

This is what followers of Jesus have always done. Followers of Jesus look to the future with eyes of hope, knowing that whatever comes their way can emerge as opportunities to bear witness to their experience of resurrection hope in Christ. We stay open to what comes our way, we cultivate reflective space to attend to what God might be inviting, and we act into the shalom of God.

It is important to remember that virtually all people in Western countries struggle with both new technology and the increasing influence of consumer culture in our lives. We encourage parents and church leaders to create experimental gatherings for the purpose of **reflecting** on how aspirations and values, not only of our young but all of us, are influenced by technology and accompanying ads that seeking to shape us twenty-four hours a day.

Finally, we urge all church leaders to recognize, as we

race into the 2020s, that we are not just facing a growing crisis of formation with Gen Next. We are also facing a crisis of formation with all generations of Christians.

All church leaders are aware of the declining levels of participation, giving, and volunteering in their settings, especially among those working-class folks who have long been the foundation of support. However, this book is written to help us recognize to what extent our aspirations and values seem to be shaped more by the aspirations and values of our Instagram-envy culture than the images of hope, hospitality, and change-making of Jesus and his community. In chapter 4, we will invite you to explore another image of the good life of God that enables us to make more time to be present to both our God and our neighbors in these troubled times. See if these images of hope begin to whet your appetite to discover more about the life God has for all of us.

Are You Ready to Be Surprised by Hope?

As followers of Jesus, our story of hope has its origins in the Old Testament vision of the shalom of God. In times like these it is essential that people of faith reconnect with this vision of hope that transcends the dominance of popular culture. We recommend reading *Shalom and the Community of Creation* by Randy Woodley. Randy, who is a First Nations missiologist, offers hope for our lives and God's good creation from a distinctly First Nations perspective that many readers will likely find refreshing. We also recommend Walter Brueggemann's *Living Towards a Vision*, in which he states, "Shalom is the substance of the biblical vision of one community embracing all creation . . . which is the vision of wholeness . . . in which persons are bound not only to God but to one another in caring, rejoicing community with none to make them afraid."[15]

Let's briefly reflect on the shalom of God's purposes for a people and our world. We will also reflect on how those aspirations and values empowered the Jewish people to live into a hope that transcended both the power of empires and the seduction of other cultures and their values.

Just over a decade ago, the gifted British New Testament scholar N. T. Wright wrote *Surprised by Hope*. He started this book not by looking ahead to some possible challenges facing society in the 2020s, but by looking back at events in the past—9/11 and Hurricane Katrina, for example—that presented those in that decade with some daunting new challenges.[16]

Wright then asks us to reflect not only on these events but also the rapidly changing contexts in other countries in that first decade of the new century: "All around, despite the heroic efforts of local leaders, there are signs of post-industrial blight, with all the human fallout of other people's power games." Wright asks the urgent question we are also asking in this book: "What hope is there for communities that have lost their way, their way of life, their coherence, and their hope?"[17]

Wright poses two foundational theological questions: "First, what is the ultimate Christian hope? Second, what hope is there for change, rescue, transformation, new

---

15. Walter Brueggemann, *Living Towards a Vision* (Cleveland: Pilgrim, 1982), 16–17.

16. N. T. Wright, *Surprised by Hope: Rethinking Heaven, the Resurrection, and the Mission of the Church* (New York: HarperCollins, 2008), 3–4.

17. Wright, *Surprised by Hope*, 5.

possibilities within the world in the present?"[18] And he finds that

> if the Christian hope is for God's new creation, for "new heavens and a new earth," and if that new hope has already come to life in Jesus of Nazareth, then there is every reason to join the two questions together. The surprising good news is that Jesus' prayer for God's kingdom to come on earth is going to be answered. At the return of Jesus, this world will be made new. We will come home not to the clouds but to a new heaven and a new earth. This world is our home, we aren't just passing through. The clouds will not be our final destination.[19]

Two of our favorite biblical images of coming home to this world "made new" are found in the imagery of that great homecoming event in Isaiah 2:1–4 and Isaiah 25:6–9.

Isaiah shares his images of the coming manifestation of the "justice and peace" of God in Isaiah 2:1–4:

> In the last days, the mountain of the Lord's temple will be established as chief among the mountains. It will be raised above the hills, and all nations will stream to it. Many peoples will come and say, "Come let us go up the mountain of the Lord, to the house of the God of Jacob. He will teach us his ways. So that we may walk in his paths." The law will go out from Zion, the word of the Lord from Jerusalem. He will judge between the nations and will settle disputes for many peoples. They will beat their swords into plowshares and their spears into pruning hooks. Nation will not take up sword against nation, nor will they train for war anymore.[20]

---

18. Wright, *Surprised by Hope*, 5.
19. Wright, *Surprised by Hope*, 5.
20. Berean Study Bible.

Now read the other imagery of the celebration into which we will all enter, into that great homecoming festival when all things are made new, in Isaiah 25:6–9:

> On that mountain the Lord Almighty will prepare a feast of food for all peoples, a banquet of aged wine, the best of meats and finest of wines. On this mountain he will destroy the shrouds that enfold all peoples, the sheets that cover all nations; he will swallow up death forever. The Sovereign Lord will wipe away the tears from all faces; he will remove the disgrace of his people from all the earth.[21]

Wright insists that this shalom future hope should be the basis of how we live, invest our lives, and offer our compassionate responses to the urgent needs that fill our world today and tomorrow: "The whole point of what Jesus was up to was that he was doing, close up, in the present, what he was promising long-term, in the future."[22] We are invited to join followers of Jesus, all over the planet, by devoting hope-filled lives and compassionate action, instead of embracing the many seductions of this new world.

Ready to Join the Mustard Seed Empire of Jesus?

Are you ready to join those laboring for a future of hope in times like these? Have you been ready? It all begins by joining those who are devoting their lives to Jesus and Jesus's compassion and hospitality, who are laboring for the

---

21. Berean Study Bible.

22. Wright, *Surprised by Hope*, 192.

mustard seed empire of Jesus that comes on a donkey's back with leftover lunches, towels, and basins.

As Trevor Malkinson reminds us:

> Jesus' use of the phrase *the kingdom of God*—his central message—had direct political connotations and implications. It was a challenge to the Empire of Rome and to all systems of domination and in general, contrasting it to what the world would be like under divine rule. . . . Crossan asserts that Jesus' metaphor of the kingdom of God was 100 percent religious and 100 percent political. William Herzog, author of *Parables as Subversive Speech*, argues that the literary turn in the interpretation of the gospels often had the result of detaching the parables from the life-world they were initially embedded in.[23]

We use the description of the coming of the mustard seed empire of Jesus because we are convinced that it is clearly both spiritual and political. One cannot read the imagery of Isaiah, where swords are transformed into plows, and not realize that in God's shalom future not only will we be changed, but the existing order will be changed as well.

Imagine for a moment the stunning spectacle of a Roman legion marching into the center of Jerusalem for a public event to reinforce the imagery of the overwhelming military power and might of the Roman Empire. Imagine some 6,000 heavily armed soldiers with helmets and body armor led by more than 300 armored soldiers on horseback. The Jewish people had a troubling history of being subjugated by the empires of Assyria, Babylon, Persia, and now Rome.

Now imagine Jesus traveling down that same exact road

---

23. Trevor Malkinson, "Thy Kingdom Come: An Analysis of the Parable of the Mustard Seed," December 2012, 10–11, https://tinyurl.com/yxycjckd.

on a donkey's back, riding alone before the crowds in *his* triumphal entry. Clearly, he was bringing not just a new spiritual order but a whole new order of human society. He embodied the images in Isaiah for the great homecoming of God!

Benedict Viviano writes, "The Kingdom of God is a new future breaking into history already present . . . especially in the ministry of Jesus Himself, yet its fullness is still to come. The divine act will be social rather than individual in character and will have its immediate political manifestations in justice and peace."[24]

When the risen Christ prepared breakfast on the beach (John 21:9–14) for those first disciples, they were experiencing a foretaste of the great homecoming banquet where we will all enjoy the best of food and best of wine. Remember, Jesus let us in on an astonishing secret. God has chosen to change the world through the lowly, the unassuming, and imperceptible. Jesus said, "What shall we say the kingdom of God is like, or what parable shall we use to describe it? It is like a mustard seed, which is the smallest of all seeds on earth. Yet when planted, it grows and becomes the largest of all garden plants, with such big branches that the birds can perch in its shade."[25]

"That has always been God's strategy—changing the world through the conspiracy of the insignificant," wrote Tom in his book. "He chose a ragged bunch of Semite slaves to become the insurgents of his new order. He chose an undersized shepherd boy with a slingshot to lead his chosen people. And who would have ever chosen to work

---

24. Benedict Viviano, *The Kingdom of God in History* (Wilmington, DE: M. Glazier, 1988), 30–31.

25. New International Version.

through a baby in a cow stall to turn this world right-side up?"[26]

Searching for Hope in the Turbulent 2020s

To become hope-filled members of the mustard seed empire of Jesus, it is urgently important to have open and clear eyes as we enter this decade of accelerating change. We recognize that churches in Western countries are likely to experience a precipitous decline in membership and reduced levels of mission-investment response across the board. As a consequence, we also need to be ready to work with and learn from the leadership of the global church that Wesley Granberg-Michaelson has predicted in *Future Faith*.

Dwight offers an important challenge for Christians in the new post-Christendom context:

> One of the unexpected gifts the post-Christendom shift seems to be offering the church is an opportunity to return to our servant role. Of course, we may reject this gift, choosing instead to maintain the comfort of church as we have known it. It is love that compels Christian hospitality and service; love of God that made evident the love of stranger; the love of God made real in serving the least.[27]

Given all the new challenges we are facing in the turbulent 2020s, we need to first recommit our lives and churches to advance the shalomic purposes of God. We need to join those who are rising to create **innovative** new ways to be a difference and make a difference in times like these. We

---

26. Sine, *The Mustard Seed Conspiracy*, 11.

27. Dwight J. Friesen, "Christian Identity Formation in a Post-Christendom Context," May 13, 2010.

invite you to join those who are already working in the 2020s to create their best lives, communities, neighborhoods, and churches.

Prayer

Triune God,

You invite us to live life and live it to the fullest. In fact, that is why you invite us to reflect on who we are becoming and what we are doing. You dare us to have courage, to act wisely, and to repent when we discover we are being malformed by values that don't reflect your shalomic imagination in the way of Jesus. You dare us to become people of faith, hope, and love. And you remind us that the greatest of these is love. Show us your love, that we may love others as we learn to love ourselves and our unique contexts. Amen.

For Group Discussion

1. Speaking of accelerating change, what are some of the challenges and opportunities that you anticipate new tech will bring to your life, family, and congregational community in the coming decade?

2. How has the Christian formation of the young changed in the past decade, given the amount of time our young spend on screens each week versus the amount of time in formation at church and at home?

3. What are the creative new ways your church is seeking to help families and particularly the young to steward new tech in their lives and relationships?

4. How is your church creating new ways for families and the congregation to do formation of Gen Next that instructs them in how to be a follower of Jesus in times like these?

5. In what specific ways is the increasingly influential advertising system using our personal data, collected by big tech, to shape our sense of what is important and of value?

6. How is the imagery of the good life and better future displayed in the world of "Instagram envy" different from the imagery we discover in the life and hospitality of Jesus and the biblical imagery of hope we witness in a world made new?

7. Is it possible for followers of Jesus, in this world of accelerating change, to reimagine and recreate new ways of housing, living, and celebrating that give fresh expression to the hope and hospitality reflected in the life and teachings of Jesus?

8. What is one imaginative way in the three-step dance (anticipate, reflect, and innovate) to reflect the hospitality and celebration of God portrayed in Isaiah 2:1–4?

Resources

Jaqueline A. Bussie, *Love Without Limits: Jesus' Radical Vision for Love with No Exceptions* (Minneapolis: Fortress Press, 2018).

David J. Lose, *Why Don't My Grandchildren Go to Church?: And What Can I Do About It?* (Minneapolis: Fortress Press, 2020).

Keith R. Anderson, *A Spirituality of Listening: Living What We Hear* (Downers Grove, IL: InterVarsity Press, 2016).

Henri J. M. Nouwen, *Discernment: Reading the Signs of Daily Life* (New York: HarperOne, 2015).

Judy Stoffel, *#LookUp: A Parenting Guide to Screen Use* (Minneapolis: Wise Ink Creative Publishing, 2019).

Dallas Willard, *Hearing God: Developing a Conversational Relationship with God* (Downers Grove, IL: InterVarsity Press, 2012)

4

Innovating for Life

My mission in life is not merely to survive, but to thrive;
and to do so with some passion, some compassion,
some humor, and some style.

—Maya Angelou

Why Settle for More and Miss the Best?

We began this journey in the first three chapters by introducing you to this new decade of accelerating change and
identifying some of the new challenges and opportunities
that we could be facing in our lives, neighborhoods, and
churches. We also showed leaders, and those they work
with, how to create innovative new responses to these
waves of change that more authentically reflect something
of God's purposes for our lives and communities.

In this chapter, we want to show leaders innovative ways
they can enable those they work with to join those who are
taking their lives back and are seeking to live into the good

life of God. We intend to offer you a way to sharpen your own sense of calling and discipline in your journey with Jesus. This chapter also provides a small-group process that will help you and others discover God's call for your own lives. We want to motivate and enable everyone to up their game in this turbulent time when we are needed the most.

Celebrating Those Going for the Best in the Olympics

The dedication and discipline of young athletes able to put aside all distractions and create a disciplined pathway to go for their very best is also a great template for spiritual formation. Here's an example:

> Ester Ledecka, a snowboarder from the Czech Republic, delivered one of the biggest upsets in Olympic history in the 2018 Olympic Games. Ledecka was the first Olympic athlete to compete in snowboarding and skiing races and was ranked 49th in the Super G and had never finished better than 19th in a World Cup race prior to the Olympics. That explained her utter shock when she was told that she had won the gold in the Super G on a pair of borrowed skis. When she saw the results on the sign that she had won the gold, she immediately went to the officials because she was convinced they had made an error. But there was no error—just a crazy, out-of-the-blue upset.[1]

If you invest in a more disciplined regime to go for your best, as followers of Jesus, like this Olympic athlete, you may be pleasantly gratified by the outcome. Another

---

1.   Josh Peter, "2018 Winter Olympics: Mikaela Shiffrin Doesn't Know if Ester Ledecka Used Her Skis," *USA Today*, February 19, 2018, https://tinyurl.com/rfa5gs9.

Olympic story from the 2018 Olympics is about a competitor from Mexico named German Madrazo, who competed in a fifteen-kilometer cross-country ski race for the first time, but he did not win the gold. In fact, he came in twenty-six minutes behind the winner.

"As weary-legged Madrazo made his final strides, he grabbed a Mexican flag . . . raised his arms in victory and got mobbed by skiers from Colombia, Morocco, Portugal, and Togo, who were all in the back of the pack, and who picked him up and carried him across the finish line."[2]

This story makes clear that going for our best does not mean expecting to win the gold in all that we do. It simply means, like Madrazo, and many others, that in times like these, we attempt, with God's help, to develop the disciplines to go for our very best in all we do. Let's revisit our three dance steps as we begin this chapter on joining those who are going for their best.

Join the Three-Step Dance

In the first two chapters, we began by focusing on step 1, **anticipating** some of the daunting waves of change heading our way in this new decade. In the third chapter, we focused more on step 2, **reflecting** on how we can disconnect our lives from the seductions of an Instagram-envy culture by reconnecting our lives more directly to God's loving purposes. In these final four chapters, we will show new ways that God is igniting our imaginations to create **innovative** ways to *be* a difference and *make* a difference in these new and exciting times.

We will offer a process to listen more carefully to God's

2. Peter, "2018 Winter Olympics."

call in our lives and invite God's spirit to ignite our imaginations with new possibilities of living in the way of Jesus with a community of friends.

This is a time for followers of Jesus to reflect on our core values and to demonstrate the hope that Jesus calls us to embrace. We have had the opportunity, in recent years, to meet and work with creative followers of Jesus all over the planet whose lives are also having an impact in a range of remarkable ways. They demonstrate what hope can look like in these rapidly changing times.

Cal and Annie: Going for Their Best in Troubled Times

We will start by introducing you to Annie and Cal, who early in their lives decided they wanted to invest themselves in going for God's best. As you will see, they and their growing family found some very innovative ways to follow Jesus, along with some new friends from Laos. Cal and Annie Uomoto not only modeled a life of hope, but also a life that reflects the hospitality of Jesus in a remarkable way.

Through their lives, Tom and some of his friends were taken on a journey of redefining what is important and what is of value. This process enabled Tom to begin redefining what the good life might look like as disciples of Jesus. This story will lead us to reflect again on the tensions we all deal with between the values of biblical faith and our increasingly influential consumer culture in the 2020s.

Tom migrated from Maui, Hawaii, to Seattle as a thirty-four-year-old. One of the first people he met when he arrived in 1970 was Cal Uomoto; they met Cal at Bethany Presbyterian Church near downtown Seattle, where they quickly became best of friends. Cal not only shared Tom's concern about our rapidly changing world, but he expanded it.

In fact, Cal became Tom's instructor regarding some of the urgent social issues facing us back in that era. For example, he introduced Tom to some of the earliest writings on the civil rights movement in the United States. Cal gave Tom a subscription to a Christian magazine that addressed some of those urgent social issues called *Post American*. Tom still has a subscription to this cutting-edge Christian magazine, now called *Sojourners*.

What attracted Tom the most to Cal and his fiancée Annie was not only their concern for new challenges facing their neighbors, but their determination as followers of Jesus to create ways to open their lives to others wherever they lived. This story really began when Cal and Annie became aware of a crisis facing Laotian farm families who began to arrive in Seattle as immigrants in the early 1970s.

These Laotian families were destitute. They were from two different tribes, the Mien and Hmong. These farm families had fought on the side of the United States in the Vietnam War. Cal explained to Tom that as the war was ending, they lost their farms and virtually everything except their lives. They were placed in refugee camps in Thailand for five years with very little hope for their futures.

Cal and Annie exchanged their vows at Bethany Presbyterian Church. Shortly after, they bought a modest three-bedroom house in a low-income, multiracial neighborhood in the Central District. It had a full basement with a bathroom plus a garage. One of the first things Cal and Annie did as newlyweds was to invite a large Laotian family to move into their basement, use their kitchen on the main floor, and enjoy life together.

Annie continued her work as a nurse and Cal completed his degree in psychology along with his master's in Administration at the University of Washington. However, Cal didn't pursue a job in administration. Instead he delivered newspapers at the University of Washington, where he had gone to school. He took this job so he could have as much free time as possible to work with Laotian families.

Cal and Annie focused their lives on the question of how to help these Laotian families to become as self-reliant as possible. First, they were joined by other volunteers from Bethany Presbyterian Church, like member Tom Lane. They devoted the next decade of their lives helping their new friends from Laos make a new beginning in Seattle. Cal and Annie persuaded King County to lease the Laotian families sixteen acres of farmland in the nearby community of Woodinville. This was an important first step.

However, as these farmers and their families soon discovered, they needed to learn a whole new form of agriculture than what they were used to in the jungles of Laos. Cal and Tom Lane found local farmers who volunteered their time and equipment to enable these Laotian farmers to make a beginning. Eventually, they learned new ways to grow vegetables and fruit on the land outside of Seattle.

One thing these Laotian farmers didn't need help with was building cooking shacks on the land where they did much of their cooking. They found scrap wood and sheet metal to construct these small shacks. Their families would celebrate on special occasions after work.

After the farm project became established, Cal and Tom worked with the leaders of the Pike Place Market, a farmers market in downtown Seattle, to rent a booth for the Laotian farmers to sell their produce on the weekends. This created other challenges. They had to teach these Laotians how to speak English and how to make change.

Over the next few years, these hard-working Laotian farmers and their families became self-reliant in ways that became a model for others working with Laotian families in other parts of the US. You can still find their vegetable and flower booths doing business in the Pike Place Market today.

This welcoming approach to hospitality became an integral part of Annie and Cal's lifestyle. They continued to host refugees not only from Laos, but from a number of other countries as well.

In 1983, the *Seattle Times* looked back at this remarkable Indochinese Farm Project. It described how these hard-working Laotian farmers and their families became self-reliant in their new lives in Seattle. The *Times* reported, "The farmers grow everything from spinach to Shanghai bok choy, cabbage, mustard greens, tomatoes, peas, Chinese parsley, and a variety of lettuces."[3] They have now expanded and are now growing a beautiful array of seasonal flowers to sell at the Pike Street Market.

Annie often reflects on the years of collaboration with these families from Laos. "It is essential that readers understand that for us this wasn't a 'service project,'" she says. "This was 'a reciprocal family project.' They lived with us, and they babysat our four sons. We gained far more than we gave." She adds, "Cal and the boys loved being a part of their harvest celebrations, where the families roasted a pig at the farm and served it with rice and stir-fried vegetables like bok choy, onions, and snow peas to express their

---

3.   Roberta Forsell, "Harvest Laotians Learn the Lay of the Land," *Seattle Times*, June 29, 1983.

appreciation for our shared family life together. We had so many memorable family times."

After Cal and Annie, their family, and friends witnessed the Laotian family's successful launch of the Farm Project, Cal took a position as the head of World Relief in Seattle, where he served for twenty-three years. During that time, he, Annie, and their family continued to enjoy sharing family life with families from all over the planet. Annie estimates they had over thirty-five families live with them.

On Sunday afternoon, November 18, 2012, Tom attended a very large memorial service for Cal Uomoto held at First Presbyterian Church. The service hosted family and friends, including the large extended family they had welcomed into their home. They came not only from Laos but from all over the world. It looked like a meeting of the United Nations. In reality, it was a wonderful celebration of this remarkable extended family coming together to express their warm appreciation to Cal and Annie.

Imagine Joining Those with a Commitment to Be a Difference and Make a Difference

We invite you to imagine what it would be like to have even a few Annies and Cals in your congregation who devote themselves in such a remarkable way, offering hospitality and joining refugees in their journey to self-reliance. We realize that not all followers of Jesus can give themselves this generously to new guests who are struggling to provide for their families in a very changing new home.

What Cal, Annie, and their sons offered was an example of a much more whole-life approach to following Jesus. For Tom, getting to know this couple was life-changing. He suspects there are people in all of our churches who might not be able to match the remarkable investment this family made but would welcome finding a path to a more serious whole-life faith.

Recall this part of my journey? By telling such stories, we want to encourage others to find serious and creative ways to up their game by the end of the 2020s. If the creative work does not happen, we could witness even more serious erosions of our churches than we witness today.

Looking Back to Discover a New Way Forward

Looking back, Tom is grateful to God for his journey with Cal and Annie and their unique approach to following Jesus, which was an important beginning for him to discover a more whole-life approach to his life of faith. It was also the beginning of a journey for him to reimagine not only his faith, but his view of what constitutes the good life as a follower of Jesus.

One of the primary teachings of Mennonite churches is a call to be whole-life disciples of Jesus, which both of us have been impacted by. This includes a commitment to a simple lifestyle, a graduated tithe, an active involvement in service in both the community and the church, and a commitment to bear witness for peace and justice issues. In the early days of our faith, we both sensed that following Jesus was more than a devotional add-on to our real lives. In different seasons in our respective journeys, we sensed we were missing out on what it meant to follow Jesus with our entire lives. Simply getting ahead in a job and increasing our ability to purchase and consume more, and attending church on Sunday, wasn't enough. We were both looking for new ways to be a difference and make a difference in this increasingly troubled world. Both Dwight and Tom were particularly impacted by the writings of authors like Ron Sider.

In 1977, Ron Sider's *Rich Christians in an Age of Hunger* exploded onto the scene. Ron Sider not only described the appalling conditions under which over a billion of our neighbors in the '70s lived on the margins, but he persuasively called people of faith to a more serious whole-life faith that focused on making a greater impact on the lives of others, just as Annie, Cal, and their sons had done.

Sider urged Christians to simplify our lifestyles and consider the radical idea of "living simply that others might simply live." He also encouraged Christians to work with those seeking to create more just political and economic systems, a very important call both then and now.

Tom started a chapter of Evangelicals for Social Action in the early '80s in Seattle. A group of about twenty people met once a month to discuss urgent needs and explore creative ways we could free up more of our resources to invest in a range of new ventures.

Ron Sider made it clear that he was not advocating we change our current economic or political systems, but rather, he was simply seeking to influence Christians of all stripes to reduce their spending on things that were not essential in order to free up more time and resources to support those working with the poor, very much what advocacy groups such as World Vision, World Concern, and Bread for the World were doing.

A number of Sider's speaking engagements at evangelical events were canceled, and he was figuratively "cast into the desert" for almost a decade, just for calling into question our society's commitment to free market economics and the individual pursuit of more. Slowly, though, even evangelical churches discovered that what Sider was calling us to was in fact a reasonable call to a more serious approach to Christian stewardship.

Sider urged Christians not simply to tithe, but to consider giving a "graduated tithe," with a generous amount going to those Christian ministries creating ways to enable our neighbors near and far to become economically self-reliant. A surprising number of Christians not only in the United States but in other Western countries started "living more simply that others might simply live."[4]

Sider also encouraged people to consider living in communities where they could reduce their lifestyles, helping one another free up time to work in local neighborhood change-making programs. In fact, from the early '70s to the mid-'80s, over a hundred such communities were started all over the United States. They not only experienced the gift of more intimate Christian communities, but they also experienced reduced lifestyle costs. One of the most satisfying aspects of shared life was, like Cal and Annie, freeing up time to work with their neighbors to plant gardens, find jobs, and become more self-reliant.

Celebrating the Good Life with Those Putting First Things First!

Following Sider's encouragement, Christians in the United States, Canada, Britain, and Australia created a range of new models of what the good life of God might look like. These communities demonstrated what family and generous hospitality could look like for followers of Jesus from all

---

4.   Ron Sider, *Rich Christians in an Age of Hunger* (Nashville: Thomas Nelson, 2005).

kinds of cultural and racial backgrounds. By living together with a common purse budget, they were able to free up a surprising amount of time and money to invest with their neighbors in community change-making. This was very radical in the '70s and it is almost unimaginable today.

One of Tom's favorite memories is of the summer gatherings of these community members, who met in a different campground in the United States every summer. Several people from Seattle would participate in these gatherings, where people would share stories of wonderful innovations that were changing their communities and neighborhoods. They also spoke about their real struggles, just like all families who are trying to make life work.

They also experienced generous times of community celebration, as the group cooked together, made music together, laughed and prayed together, and got a little taste of living in the way of Jesus. If you would like to get a more complete picture of those days of followers of Jesus "living simply that others might simply live," read the book *Living Together in a World Falling Apart* by Dave and Neta Jackson.

Communities Today Still Celebrating the Good Life of God

Thankfully, there are still remnants of this community network alive and functioning, from Reba Place and Jesus People USA to the Community of Transfiguration in Australia and the Taizé Community in France.

In the last two decades Tom has been inspired by examples of the New Monasticism Movement created by Shane Claiborne and Jonathan Wilson-Hartgrove. These two vital new communities, the Simple Way and the Rutba Community, are still going strong. (Of course, a number of Catholic orders have been around for centuries. Regrettably, their numbers seem to be declining as well.)

Ched Myers, who was part of a Christian movement in the '80s, has in recent years created a new movement that includes a fresh approach to creation care and a more whole-life approach to discipleship, called Watershed Discipleship. Check out the website at www.watersheddiscipleship.org.

Ched, who heads this website, encourages us to view our marvelous created world through the eyes of First Nations peoples. They view the watershed that supports their life and all the life around them as a sacred place. Most of us in Western countries don't even know which watersheds support our lives.

Also, check out a new movement started by leaders from Gen Y and Z called "Young Evangelicals for Climate Action." Here is their Faithful Action Pledge:

> We are young evangelicals striving to live out what Jesus said was most important: loving God fully and loving our neighbors as ourselves. Climate change is already impacting our neighbors and God's creation here in the United States and around the world. For the sake of "the least of these," we believe God is calling us to faithful action and witness in the midst of the current climate crisis. Therefore, we commit ourselves to living faithfully as good stewards of creation, advocating on behalf of the poor and marginalized, supporting our faith and political leaders when they stand up for climate action, and mobilizing our generation to join in.[5]

---

5. Young Evangelicals for Climate Action, www.yecaction.org.

As we will discuss in the next chapter on "creating your best communities," there is an opportunity for all of us, but particularly young innovators, to create new communities that give innovative expression to what the good life of Jesus could look like in the turbulent 2020s through new shared-living models. This generation of young innovators can turn their struggle with escalating school debt and rising housing prices toward creating a spectrum of new shalom communities that artfully display what the good life of God could look like in these times.

We do not share these ideas to suggest we should return to the past. Rather, they are shared to urge leaders of all kinds to get acquainted with a range of new co-living and intergenerational communities today, which we will explore in the next chapter. These new options provide new, less expensive housing options for both the young and many of us who are older on fixed incomes. However, like the common purse communities of the '70s and '80s, they could also enable disciples of all ages to free up more time and resources. Those resources could be invested in neighborhood change-making and generous hospitality.

Reflection: What Is the Good Life You Want to Pursue in the 2020s?

We know that many leaders are increasingly concerned by the declining participation of core members of their congregations and key supporters of nonprofits. This is why we are focusing on the question "What is the good life?" We are encouraging you and those you work with to reflect on the values we live by, individually and as families.

In the last chapter, we asked: "Where do we find hope

in times like these?" We discovered advertisers are working overtime to convince us that *they* are the merchants of hope. Charles Revson, the founder of Revlon, once said, "In our factories we make lipstick. In our advertising we sell hope."[6]

We also discovered in *The Age of Surveillance Capitalism* that advertisers are collecting and selling an amazing amount of personal data about us and our kids. As we have seen, the view of the best life they are trying to sell us and our youth is an endless pursuit of more than we can afford. And we noted how the amount of screen time most of us and our youth pursue daily could be leading to a crisis of formation.[7] By formation here we mean choosing the ideas, beliefs, and values that inform where live, how we steward our time and resources, and even how we celebrate life. We want you to reflect critically on what it is that forms your aspirations and values and those you work with.

Invitation to Reflect on What Shapes Our View of What Is the Good Life

James K. A. Smith, in his important book *You Are What You Love*, encourages us to be aware of what we love and who convinced us to buy into our notions of the good life. He states, "We need to become aware of our immersions: 'This is the water' you've been swimming in your whole life. We need to recognize that our imaginations and longings are not impervious to our environments nor informed solely by our (supposedly 'critical') thinking." Smith insists, "To the contrary, our loves and imaginations are conscripted by all

---

6. M. T. Wroblewski, reviewed by Michelle Seidel, "How Does Advertising Influence People?," *Houston Chronicle*, updated January 24, 2019.

7. Zuboff, *The Age of Surveillance Capitalism.*

sorts of liturgies that are loaded with a vision of the good life."[8]

Is Smith right? Is our notion of the good life largely shaped by "the water we have been swimming in"? Wesley Granberg-Michaelson writes about this in *Future Faith*: "Western culture, shaped by the Enlightenment, has become the comfortable home for the dominant expressions of Christianity in the world."[9]

Most Christian leaders we have worked with, from a broad spectrum of traditions, have thoughtfully developed theological worldviews. However, sometimes we have not always developed a way to see the intersection of our theological assumptions and the popular cultural assumptions that we are immersed in.

One of the growing influences of the Enlightenment has been the development of a new self-interested economic theory. John B. Cobb Jr., in an article titled "Consumerism, Economism and Christian Faith," explains that during the Enlightenment our view of greed was revised. "David Hume . . . argued for the positive social value of commerce based on the profit motive, although he feared unadulterated greed, and thought in commerce it was mixed with other motives."[10]

Adam Smith, author of *The Wealth of Nations*, is quoted in the article saying that "the market works best when each participant acts in terms of rational self-interest."[11] Smith's view seemed to suggest that if we all could simply pursue

---

8. James K. A. Smith, *You Are What You Love: The Spiritual Power of Habit* (Grand Rapids: Brazos, 2016), 38.

9. Wesley Granberg-Michaelson, *Future Faith: Ten Challenges Reshaping Christianity in the 21st Century* (Minneapolis: Fortress Press, 2017), 2.

10. John B. Cobb Jr., "Consumerism, Economism and Christian Faith," Religiononline.org.

11. Cobb, "Consumerism, Economism and Christian Faith."

our own self-interests, the world will all come up roses for everyone.

Cobb observes that most Christians in America today have moved from modest consumerism to an increasing appetite for more: "Most of us expect to have more space in our homes, more toilets, more electronic equipment, more varied food, better automobiles, more vacation travel, and larger wardrobes that seem to require closets the size of small bedrooms that we didn't seem to need to two or three decades ago."[12] Remember, big tech is selling our personal information, and advertisers are becoming more effective in selling us their version of hope based on an increasingly self-interested life.

"Stop Trying to Raise Successful Kids" is an article in *The Atlantic* that challenges parents who are seeking to raise kids to believe that going for their best is enabling their children to be economically successful. "Kids learn what's important to adults not by listening to what they say, but by noticing what gets our attention. And in many developed societies, parents pay more attention to individual achievement and happiness than anything else. However much we praise kindness and caring, we're not actually showing our kids that we value these traits."[13]

"Perhaps we shouldn't be surprised that kindness seems to be in decline. A rigorous analysis of an annual survey of college students showed a substantial drop from 1979 to 2009 in empathy and in imagining the perspectives of others. Over this period, students grew less likely to feel concern for people less fortunate than themselves—and less

12.   Cobb, "Consumerism, Economism and Christian Faith."

13.   Adam Grant and Allison Sweet Grant, "Stop Trying to Raise Successful Kids and Start Raising Kind Ones," *The Atlantic*, December 2019, 36.

bothered by seeing people being treated unfairly."[14] Shouldn't followers of Jesus embrace a view of the good life of God that is focused on kindness and empathy instead of individual acquisition of more? Shouldn't Christian parents be offering a different message than what kids are bombarded with on their many screens?

Doesn't our imagery of the good life largely define how we use our time, our money, and even where we work? Will it define how we raise our kids and plot the future that you attempt to help them achieve? Will it determine whether you will take time with friends to grow your relationship with the Creator, or join those making a difference in your neighborhood? Wouldn't this also help you define how much time the people you lead may spend investing in the servanthood values of Jesus?

Most of us start our lives with good dreams and with all the best intentions, and yet, many of us wind up with something very different from our best dreams. The very good news is that it is never too late to start over. It is never too late to discover what God's best might be for you at this stage of life.

We want to help you and those you work with to discern a clearer sense of vocation for your life, just as Annie and Cal did. We wish you and those you love a way of life that reflects something of the hospitality of Jesus in times like these. Remember, as you begin your Quest for the Best, God specializes in using our ordinary lives to make a difference in the lives of others.

---

14.   Grant and Grant, "Stop Trying," 36.

Reflecting on the Way of Jesus

The Jesus who rides comes on a donkey's back comes announcing the good news of the empire of the mustard seed. The even better news is that God can use our individual lives to bring real change in the lives of others, who, in turn, will change our lives too. We each can be used in ways we have not yet imagined. Remember, Jesus hung out with tax collectors and women when it wasn't socially acceptable. He demonstrated the importance of hospitality and actually created a new kind of family.

Even though the powerful Roman Empire dominated Jerusalem and the surrounding regions, Jesus made it clear that Rome would not have the final word. Jesus reminded his listeners where they would find hope. He told them that not only is God alive and well, but God's shalom purposes welcome us to that great homecoming celebration where all things are made new.

Richard Middleton and Bryan Walsh state that

> Jesus came rejecting "the world of grasping" that characterized his age and ours and affirms the world of the gift. He comes as an agent of this new kingdom, dispensing gifts to those who are dispossessed. His ministry of healing, exorcism, and table fellowship, and teaching restored the broken, freed the oppressed, welcomed the outcast, and taught a new pathway home.[15]

In his inspiring book *Whole and Reconciled*, Al Tizon, who heads Serve Globally for the Covenant Church, challenges readers to discover in scripture an alternative vision of the

---

15.   J. Richard Middleton and Brian J. Walsh, *Truth Is Stranger Than It Used to Be: Biblical Faith in a Postmodern Age* (Downers Grove, IL: InterVarsity Press, 1995), 161.

good life of God that is found more in making a difference in the lives of others than in pursuing a life of acquisition. He quotes Rene Padilla, who calls all Christians "to embrace an alternative lifestyle centered in the kingdom of God and [God's] community-restoring justice, which brings peace to the poor and oppressed."[16]

Examples of Those Innovating for Their Best

In a moment, we will outline a simple pathway that you and a few friends can use to design a plan to create your best life. But first, we share some examples of people who have created new pathways to a life that better reflects the way of Jesus. These disciples of Christ are creating innovative models of whole-life faith that we need to see more of in the 2020s.

Hospitality Family Calling

Tim and Katey, a young couple with three elementary-age kids, live outside of Chicago. They were part of a small group that used our discernment process at their Presbyterian church to create a pathway for their family to create their best life.

After the series of discernment meetings in which participants reflected on scripture about the topics of welcoming God to the needs of their neighborhood, and after much discussion and prayer, Katey and Tim felt a strong calling to embody the hospitality of God in their neighborhood. Once a week, each of their children would select a different

---

16. Al Tizon, *Whole and Reconciled: Gospel, Church, and Mission in a Fractured World* (Grand Rapids: Baker, 2018), 14–15.

neighbor to have over for dinner. Some of the families they invited had kids their age; others didn't have kids at all.

Their new family mission statement included their kids learning to develop the gift of hospitality. Kathy and Tim invited kids to offer ideas for these fellowship evening meals and enlisted their help in preparing it. The three kids not only set the table and helped with cleanup, they also learned to be vigilant in watching and quickly responding to the needs of their guests. Their parents told us this experience made their whole family much more attentive to the interests and needs of others in all of their relationships. Becoming the hospitality of Jesus became part of the lives of each member in the family.

Housing Refocused

Lisa and Bill took a seminary course together on faith and money that led them to reflect out of their biblical faith how they wanted to steward all the resources in their lives, including their housing. Essentially, they developed a plan for whole-life stewardship. They chose to limit their lifestyle costs by rapidly paying off what they initially purchased as a small, relatively inexpensive starter house. Lisa and Bill decided to use the money they freed up to devote more time to enabling their poorer neighbors to find ways to become more self-reliant.

Empowering Kids with Disabilities

Ivan was a businessman in Australia. He confessed that he was overwhelmed by his business and by his own sense of brokenness. In his quest to discover his best life while attending a small group at his church, he drafted a mission statement that read: "I commit my life to partnering with God, to projecting God's love to the unloved." Ivan started using his leisure time to work with children living with disabilities, even passing up promotions to free up time for ministry. He and his wife started a small business to enable them to free up more time for the kids. Ivan says that "the good life of God is indeed the life given away."[17]

Do these stories encourage you? Do you have people in your congregation, campus ministry, or maybe even in your workplace who might be interested in being part of a group attempting to create a more focused way of life where they carve out time to focus on the things that matter most as followers of Jesus? Recently, we found a remarkable new movement in colleges across America called Life Design, which is empowering students to go for their best by creating a way of life to make a difference.

Learning from the "Life Design" Movement to Go for Our Best!

Silicon Valley veterans Dave Evans and Bill Burnett started the Designing Your Life Seminar at Stanford University. Evans and Burnett's 2016 book *Designing Your Life* quickly became a *New York Times* bestseller. Remarkably, versions of that course have spread to universities all over the United States.

One of the reasons it is connecting with students has to do with some of the unique passions, concerns, and fears of Gen Z that we have already mentioned. Many in both Gen Y and Z are deeply concerned about the escalating environ-

---

17.   Sine, *Mustard Seed Versus McWorld*.

mental crisis and the issues of racial and economic justice as we race into the 2020s. Many in Gen Z are also feeling very overwhelmed because they don't feel equipped to deal with all the rapid changes as they launch their lives in the 2020s.

Many Life Design courses "that have sprung up on campuses are deliberately geared toward addressing the challenges and opportunities awaiting them in an unknown future. They are built around 'design thinking,' which is a problem-solving approach in the tech world that has moved into the mainstream in the past few years."[18]

These courses are designed not only to reduce a student's fear of failure but to help them discover that when they don't succeed on one pathway, it simply means that they need to try a different route. Even though these courses are not "religious," they often use terms like *vocation* and *calling*. Instructors emphasize that Life Design is not about choosing a career. It is about moving away from a self-interested life and designing a purposeful and meaningful way of life that makes a difference in the world.[19] Perhaps drawing on a bit of the Life Design model might be a good place to begin in our churches and neighborhoods to connect to those in Gen Y and Z.

In this proposed "Quest for the Best" workshop below, we are attempting to offer a pathway to reimagine how to order our lives, like Cal and Annie and the other examples we briefly shared, to go for our very best lives, refocusing in these turbulent times. We offer this workshop to you to use with a small group in your church or community that might be interested in going for their best life.

---

18.   Stephanie Hanes, "campuses:YOU," *Christian Science Monitor*, December 9, 2019, 26.

19.   Hanes, "campuses:YOU," 29.

Starting a *Quest for the Best* Group

As Canadian songwriter Bruce Cockburn says in the opening line of his song "Laughter," "Tried to build the New Jerusalem and ended up with New York."[20] Know the feeling? In our quest for the best, it is easy to wind up being sidetracked and settle for less!

Those of you in leadership have probably met a number of followers of Jesus who started with good dreams and much enthusiasm and have gotten sidetracked and settled for much less than their best. Of course, some people are boxed in and are not in a place where they can even reimagine how they might refocus. However, others are more than ready to explore ways of refocusing their lives and join those going for their best. Do you have a small group of laity in your congregation, or in some other setting, that might be motivated to "up their game" and go for their best life? Here is one process that you and those you work with might find helpful. We would value learning how it works for you and your community. We would value hearing from people who actually launched their Quest for the Best ideas and how their new ventures are taking off.

In whatever context you find yourself, we encourage you to bring together a small group of five or seven people who are open to a process of joining a quest to create their best lives. In these turbulent times, reach out to people who are searching for ways to refocus their lives and even their family or community.

The purpose of your Quest for the Best life group is four-fold:

---

20.   Christine and Tom Sine, *Living on Purpose: Finding God's Best for Your Life*, (Baker Books, 2002), 11.

1. To identify areas of life that may be holding us back from fully following the way of Jesus, which may include the dramatic pressures imposed by our rapidly accelerating culture, and to examine these issues critically in the light of scripture and through additional reading and mutual conversation;

2. To identify new ways the Creator God can use our ordinary lives to join with others, to both be a difference and make a little difference that reflects something of the ways of Jesus, engaging tomorrow's new challenges in ways that reflect hope-filled possibilities for these divided times;

3. To discern how the shalom purposes of God reflected in the life of Jesus and that first community can enable us to discern a new focus for our lives and families . . . that call us beyond the aspirations of our consumer culture;

4. To research, with others, innovative ways to both be a difference and make a difference as we learn to anticipate, ways that reflect both the compassion and creativity of the followers of Jesus for times like these.

These purposes will be worked out as we join others in pursuing new ways of living together and carving out daily time to be present to God. We will carve out weekly time to be involved with others in creating ways to make a difference in our communities. Finally, we also take time, like that early community of Jesus, to offer hospitality and throw better parties that celebrate the reality that we serve a God who is committed to making all things new.

Suggested Format for a Quest for the Best Group

The following process can be done in six to seven sessions of about ninety minutes. We recommend that each session begin with a time of prayer followed by a time of response to one or more key questions. As the sessions proceed, time for reflecting on scripture and individual sharing of concerns and creative plans will become the primary activity. Alert the group that some amount of individual research and planning may be needed as preparation for the next group meeting.

Session 1: Taking a Look at Where We Are

- Begin with prayer.
- Introduce the reason this group is gathered. Refer as needed to the fourfold purpose above. Remind the group that they are engaging in a process of mutual sharing, support, and discernment to identify what "going for the best" might look like for each participant's life. Conversations that take place in the group can be sensitive, and confidentiality is to be respected.
- Consider starting by providing participants an informal opportunity to get acquainted with some refreshments. Before they share anything about their reasons for joining this Quest for the Best group, you might start with an informal "getting acquainted" time. You might have everyone share one of their favorite things and then simply invite participants to get acquainted over munchies and beverages. When they are done, you might invite them to share a bit of what they learned about others they talked to.

- Now invite participants to share why they chose to participate in a Quest for the Best group by identifying what they are hoping for in this process. Have participants share a few more details about their lives, their relationships, their work. Make sure each participant has the opportunity to share not only what they are struggling with but what "the best" is that they are aspiring to in times like these, with God's help. Be sure to get a little clearer sense of what they hope to derive from this time together.

- Write the following questions on chart paper and instruct participants to write brief responses on sticky notes that they will affix to each question.

1. List some of the new challenges you and your partner or family are likely to face in the next three to five years. This may include challenges you currently are facing. You may refrain from listing things you feel are too sensitive. Think about what makes these things a challenge or barrier to living your best life as a follower of Jesus.

2. Briefly describe a beginning vision of what your best life could be, or list three things that may be most needed for you to create your best life.

- After participants have placed their sticky notes on the charts, take some time to review the comments aloud. At this point the responses are relatively anonymous. Ask individuals to comment on their responses if they wish. After this discussion has run its course, ask the group to observe some of the common concerns, themes, and needs listed.

- Read Psalm 139:1–6 and ask participants to reflect on the text. What images, words, or phrases have meaning for them? What connection do they see between the text and imagining their best lives as God's people?

- As an assignment, ask each person to think about the concerns they identified during the coming week. Ask them also to think about:

1. What are likely to be new challenges facing their neighbors or community today?

2. What are likely to be some new challenges facing them in the next five years?

3. What are some creative new ways that you or others in your church might respond to these challenges?

4. What are some other concerns locally or globally that God seems to be stirring in your heart, and how do you sense you would like to be involved with others in responding to these challenges through your discretionary time? Your work time?

5. What would it take for you to move forward by collaborating with others to create new forms of change-making for times like these?

6. How would you need to make some lifestyle or time-style changes to have time each day to be present to God and time each week to be involved with others in local change-making?

7. Your assignment for Session 2 next week: What are some of the elements in popular culture that tend to distance you from going for your best, that we discuss later in this chapter? What are the scripture texts that seem to motivate you to go for your very

best? Bring one or two of the most compelling to share next week. Also, who are several people you could invite to join you in discerning ways you could create your best life in times like these? Be prepared to share some reflections in the group at the next session.

Session 2: Turbulent Times Ready or Not!

Start this session with prayer and then invite people to reflect on the first session and any new ideas or questions it raised for them based on the first session:

1. Where do you sense, after our first session, God might be encouraging you to join with others, during your discretionary time or your work time, to be more involved in some form of change-making? How might you modify your daily schedule to free up time to be more present to God through scripture and prayer?

2. Since our first session, where did you discover ways that popular culture is influencing your aspirations and values that in turn tend to influence how you steward both your time and resources? Finally, what scripture texts most compellingly motivate you to create a new pathway to go for your very best? These scriptures will become key as you define a clearer sense of how you feel called to be a follower of Jesus in times like these.

In this second session, we will focus on **anticipating** new challenges and opportunities that are likely to face you, as well as your friends and neighbors, in the coming decade.

Start with some of the challenges mentioned in the first three chapters of the book. What are some other challenges you see that could impact you, your children, your friends, or your neighbors?

In attempting to discern your Quest for the Best, it is essential to not only identify scripture that calls you beyond yourself to join those who are making a difference. It is also essential to discern what are the needs around you today and in our rapidly changing tomorrows that seem to stir your heart. Those stirrings could be a part of God's call to join those addressing some important new needs and opportunities. So be sure to write these stirrings along with those scriptures that call you beyond yourself.

For any college students in your group, it might be an opportunity to begin exploring vocational options, such as the life design classes (mentioned earlier) that engage issues they deeply care about.

- Ask participants to come prepared to share some additional new opportunities that they, their churches, or communities could be facing in the next five years and innovative ways that they or churches in their community might respond.

Session 3: God's Plans, Our Plans

- Begin your session with prayer. If participants are comfortable praying, invite them to offer prayers aloud.

- Take some time for participants to share some of their reflections done during the preceding week. How are they viewing the challenges differently? Have they discovered any information that helps or increases their anxiety? Did they think about who might be helpful conversation partners as they imagine their best lives?

- Read and reflect on the following scripture passages: Luke 4:14–19 and 1 Corinthians 1:26–30. Ask what words, images, or phrases have meaning for participants. How does each passage provide a vision of God's purposes and guidance for following your best life as a follower of Jesus? What is surprising about these texts, and how might that speak to the pressures and challenges imposed by our accelerated world?

- Ask participants to share examples of people who, like Cal, Annie, and so many others, have discovered that the good life of God is found in the life given away. Ask them to share what their sense of going for their best looked like. Be sure to have them share the difference it made in their communities and in the lives of others.

- Invite any comments on these examples. Ask participants to share any additional examples of people they have read about or know. What is it about these people that inspires them?

- Next, turn to the key activity of having each participant think creatively about how they will create a plan to guide their design of their own best life as a follower of Jesus. Ask them: What are your dreams for going for your best life, and what are your first steps to get started? Be sure that they identify the new need or opportunity they feel called to join others in addressing and to write down the scriptures that most compellingly call them beyond themselves. Also encourage them to write some ideas down in a journal and to think about who will support them in creating and living out their plan. After some time for individual work, ask participants to share their initial thoughts with one conversation partner.

- After a time for one-on-one conversation, gather the group together. Engage in another time of prayer, focusing specifically on the plans being created.

- As an assignment for the coming week, ask participants to continue reflecting on their plans and making them more concrete. In the next session, they will share their initial plans with the whole group.

Session 4: Expanding Our Plans

- Begin with prayer.

- Ask participants to share their initial creative thinking about their Quest for the Best life plans. After everyone has shared with the group, invite supportive comments or questions. Focus on encouragement rather than critique. Remind them that this is only the first step toward a plan.

- After a time of sharing, read the following scripture together: Isaiah 42:5–9. Ask participants to identify words, phrases, or images that are particularly meaningful. Where have they heard this vision of justice before? What "new things" might God be declaring in their lives? In the world?

- Then move to another exercise with chart paper and sticky notes. Remind the group that up to this point, we have been focusing primarily on our own lives and plans.

1. How will they need to change their time-styles and lifestyles to carve out time either through their discretionary time or their work time to join others in investing their life in ways that empower others and make a difference in communities?

2. Who will you join in your Quest for the Best, or who do you hope will join you in this venture? Where will you secure the needed resources? Where will you locate others from your church or community to join you?

3. How will you and your collaborators evaluate your project quarterly?

4. When will you plan a celebration each year to express appreciation for all those who are involved?

- As an assignment for the next session, ask participants to review their initial Quest for the Best life plans alongside the broader community concerns and opportunities identified in this session. Ask them to focus on specific ways their best-life plans could intersect with these broader concerns and opportunities. How might their best-life plans be modified? Ask them to write their thoughts in a journal and be prepared to share at the next session.

We always need to start with the first and second great commandments: "Jesus replied: 'Love the Lord your God with all your heart and with all your soul and with all your mind.' This is the first and greatest commandment. And the second is like it: 'Love your neighbor as yourself.' All the Law and the Prophets hang on these two commandments."[21] Going for our best then

---

21.   Matthew 22:37–40, New International Version.

becomes a creative opportunity to change our time-styles and lifestyles so we have daily time to be present with God and discover ways every week to care for our neighbors. We encourage each group leader to enable participants to discern passages that speak directly to them in their quest for the best life as followers of Jesus.

Session 5: Creating Your Best Life for Today and Tomorrow

- Begin with prayer.

- Ask participants to share their additional creative thinking about their best-life plans. After everyone has shared with the group, invite supportive comments or questions. Focus on encouragement rather than critique.

- Read and reflect on the following scripture passage: Matthew 6:25–34. What words, images, or phrases are particularly meaningful? Part of the premise of this book is that we need to be aware of the future and the problems tomorrow may bring. How does this square with Jesus's words: "Do not worry about tomorrow, for tomorrow will bring worries of its own"? How do you see God's righteousness connected to worry and challenges placed on us by the world?

- One of the significant challenges we face as we imagine innovative ways to refocus our lives is what this may mean for our schedules and how we prioritize our time. Ask participants to think about their Quest for the Best life plans in relation to discovering ways to reinvent their time-styles and lifestyles that are sustainable.

- Begin to think about how you will celebrate this new Quest for the Best life plan with others.

Session 6: Sharing Our Plans Together

- Begin with prayer.
- Have participants take turns sharing their plans to pursue their Quest for the Best life plans in the turbulent 2020s. How will they reorder their schedules and lifestyles to pursue the plan? Who will be part of their support team? End each presentation with a time of prayer and laying on of hands.
- When all have presented, ask participants to imagine how they can support one another. After a time of sharing, you could suggest the following:

  Go on a retreat with your partner or a friend and work together to develop a realistic plan by setting goals for the next four months. (Tom reports that he and his wife Christine go on two-day prayer retreats quarterly. It helps them keep their goals in mind and also lead a more festive, balanced life. They also journal each Sunday before they go to worship service and share how they are doing on their journey with one another. They find it is always helpful to start by writing and sharing what they are most grateful for to God and one another in the past week. Then, they set goals for the week ahead.)

  We strongly suggest "alumni meetings" of this group set for two to four months in the future to share stories of both struggle and blessing. How are their new ventures in creating best lives in times like these going? Talk about how you can celebrate, and share your experience more widely to encourage others who are struggling in these turbulent and seductive times.

- Close this session by reading the following scripture: Psalm 121.

- End the session with prayer that all will find a clear sense of calling as followers of Jesus, and that all can both *be* a difference and *make* a difference in response to the growing challenges in the 2020s. Pray that all may reflect God's shalom and discover the focus and discipline of Olympic athletes, so they can run their best race in times like these.

Session 7: Celebrating Our Quest for the Best Life Plans (optional)

- Begin your celebration with a prayer of thanksgiving.

- Share both your struggles and what you and your community have done to make a little difference.

- Be sure to express sincere gratitude for all of those involved.

- Enjoy laughter over every stumble and blind alley.

- Share and celebrate all your plans for new ways forward.

- Take time to worship the God of all new beginnings and pray for wisdom for new ways forward in the coming year.

Prayer

Source of Life,

Jesus once said that he came to give life, life to the full. Yet, sometimes, it feels like we are just putting in time, or even worse, wasting our time on things that are not priorities. Sometimes, we wonder whether our lives matter. The little boy who offered his lunch to Jesus to feed the five thousand likely never knew that his act of offering what he had would be remembered centuries later. Help us to see what is in our hands; what is ours to give, use, or offer. Help us to listen, wonder, and risk taking one little step of faithfulness. That's all. God, today, help me to be in the moment. Help me to live a life that says yes to you and to all my neighbors. Amen.

For Group Discussion

1. As you read about students in colleges all over the country seeking a focus not only to make a living but to also design their lives to make a difference, what possibilities did that raise for you?

2. As you read the descriptions of what a life designed to make a difference looked like for Annie and Cal Uomoto, and the other brief examples, what questions and possibilities began to stir for you?

3. How did this chapter connect to the biblical images of hope for you that we explored in chapter 3? What images or verses of Scripture seem to particularly call you beyond yourself?

4. In what ways did the last chapter on biblical hope and this chapter on going for your best also begin

to create new images for you of what the good life might look for followers of Jesus in times like these?

5. As you worked through the Quest for the Best Process, did you begin to explore a possible new focus in designing ways you could become more directly involved in hope-making and change-making through your career or discretionary time?

6. Who would you need to collaborate with and in what time frame to design your Best Life for these turbulent times?

7. What changes would you need to make with others and in your time-styles and lifestyles to pursue your Quest for the Best? How might you free up time and resources to have more time for neighbors and God?

8. What kinds of celebrations might you create, with all those involved, to celebrate the in-breaking of God's hope in your lives, your neighborhood, or your church?

Resources

James K. A. Smith, *You Are What You Love: The Spiritual Power of Habit* (Grand Rapids: Brazos, 2016).

D. L. Mayfield, *The Myth of the American Dream: Reflections on Affluence, Autonomy, Safety and Power* (Downers Grove, IL: InterVarsity Press, 2020).

Bill Burnett and Dave Evans, *Designing Your Life: How to Build a Well-Lived, Joyful Life* (New York: Knopf, 2016).

Mark Scandrette, *Free: Using Your Time and Money for What*

Matters Most (Downers Grove, IL: InterVarsity Press, 2016).

Mark and Lisa Scandrette, *Belonging and Becoming: Creating a Thriving Family Culture* (Downers Grove, IL: InterVarsity Press, 2016).

Christine Sine, *The Gift of Wonder: Creative Practices for Delighting in God* (Downers Grove, IL: InterVarsity Press, 2018).

Christine Sine and Tom Sine, *Living on Purpose: Finding God's Best for Your Life* (Grand Rapids: Baker, 2002).

Samuel Wells, *A Nazareth Manifesto: Being with God* (Hoboken, NJ: Wiley, 2015).

Young Evangelicals for Climate Action, https://www.yecaction.org/.

5

Innovating for Community-Making

There is no power for change greater than a community discovering what it cares about.

—Margaret J. Wheatley

Celebrating Community Renewal in Lake Hills

Shortly after Dwight and his wife, Lynette, moved into Bellevue's Lake Hills neighborhood, the Texaco station at the center of their community's shopping district burned entirely to the ground. Fortunately, no one was hurt, but the charred remains of the service station left a scar on the psyche of the community, as it sat crumbling for nearly a decade.

Eventually, the remains of the building were torn down and a predictably obnoxious chain-link fence was installed, rendering the lot entirely unusable for the neighborhood.

No Trespassing signs were posted. Weeds grew. Trash piled up. And that abandoned empty corner lot began negatively shaping the internal narrative of Lake Hills' residents.

Every spring, Dwight and Lynette, with the help of their neighbors, threw a crawfish boil. Dwight was elbow deep in crawfish one year when he began asking the crew what they thought about that vacant lot. Everyone agreed that something needed to be done. Together, they decided to spread the word that there would be a planning meeting at the neighborhood coffee shop to develop their strategy. The scheming of a small group of neighbors led to the idea to "yarn bomb" the fence.

They mobilized a Girl Scout troop, recruited crafty folks through social media to crochet colorful flowers, and brought in others from different faith communities and cultural backgrounds in the neighborhood. When the agreed-upon day arrived, the residents gathered together and reactivated the once-vacant lot. They weeded and trimmed trees and shrubs. They recycled trash and covered the sidewalk with chalk art. And most importantly, they drew attention to the lot by transforming the ugly chain-link fence into a mini-work of yarn-bombed art.

The fence came alive with hundreds of colorful crocheted flowers, bright ribbons streaming the whole length of the fence, and a large sign with vibrant lettering that read, "We Love Lake Hills!"

Rather than being the blight of neighborhood, now the lot was drawing good attention. It got people talking, even wondering: if neighbors were invested in this corner to such a degree that all this work could be accomplished, then just *maybe* that corner lot might be worth redeveloping. And sure enough, just a few months after the neighbors reactivated that corner lot, a plan was brought forward to reimagine the site for businesses that now serve the Lake Hills neighborhood.

What these Lake Hills residents did was a form of Guerilla Urbanism.[1] Innovating for community can begin with small acts, like beautifying an ugly chain-link fence together with a diverse group of neighbors. Often the impetus to innovate for community emerges from crises or conflicts. Who knew that a burnt-down Texaco station could band people together? But it did.

Dancing the Three-Step to Create Your Best Community-Making in the 2020s

Can you imagine joining your neighbors in creating new forms of God's abundant life where you live? Communities often face waves of change, so it is essential for leaders to learn to anticipate these incoming waves of change so they have time to both reflect on their purposes and research best practices of **innovative** ways to join others in responding to these new opportunities.

Step One: Anticipating

We urge leaders and those they work with to identify community-making opportunities that bring together neighbors to create more compassionate, resilient communities for these challenging times.

We need to wake up to the opportunities evident today

---

1. For more ideas like this, and ways you can help mobilize your neighbors to make your built environment reflect your communities' dreams, check out Mike Lydon, Anthony Garcia, et al., *Tactical Urbanism: Short-Term Action for Long-Term Change* (Washington, DC: Island Press, 2015).

and anticipate those that are just over the horizon. And that involves casting our eyes to new opportunities that lie all around us. Leonard Cohen once said that there is a crack in everything . . . that's how the light gets in.[2] We need leaders looking for those cracks. We need "to let the light shine in" by enabling those we work with to identify promising new possibilities for our neighborhood and our neighbors in the 2020s. For example, leaders need to anticipate the epidemic of homelessness we could face in the next ten years.

Step 2: Reflection

In *Making Room: Recovering Hospitality as a Christian Tradition*, Christine D. Pohl reminds us, "That writers in the New Testament portray Jesus as a gracious host, welcoming children and prostitutes, tax collectors and sinners into his presence. . . . Jesus knew the vulnerability of the homeless infant, the child refugee, the adult with no place to lay his head, the despised convict."[3]

Pohl adds, "Early Christian hospitality was offered from within the overlap of household and church . . . the church was a new household, and believers became family to one another."[4] Even more remarkable, this first-century church not only became family, but believers from different political, ethnic, and socioeconomic backgrounds actually became family. Is this still possible for faith communities today?

Community leaders have much to learn from the hos-

---

2.   Leonard Cohen, "Anthem," *The Future*, Columbia, 1992, track 5.

3.   Christine D. Pohl, *Making Room: Recovering Hospitality as a Christian Tradition* (Grand Rapids: Eerdmans, 1999), 16–17.

4.   Pohl, *Making Room*, 42–43.

pitality extended by Jesus and the early church. In these challenging times, we need to shift from a model of token charity to working with neighbors to create serious new models of community hospitality and change-making that reflect God's great shalom.

Step 3: Creating Our Best Communities

The third step of the dance will involve actively joining those that are researching a broad range of **innovative** approaches to housing as well as new forms of community hospitality and empowerment. It is also an opportunity to get friends and neighbors to join creative neighborhood change-making, like the regenerative processes modeled by Dwight and Lynnette and their community in the Lake Hills neighborhood.

Anticipating Divisive Times and Challenging Housing Times in the Troubled 2020s

As we gallop into this new decade, we are experiencing an accelerating level of divisiveness not only in our politics but in our communities, in many of our churches, and even in our families. How can people of faith find ways to be agents of reconciliation instead of unwitting agents of division?

Marc Dunkelman says in his book *The Vanishing Neighbor: The Transformation of American Community*, "These divisive times come with huge social costs. A growing number of Americans are increasingly hanging out with those that share their fears and anger." Some are reportedly succumbing to conspiracy theories about other groups that only increase their fear and anger. Dunkelman continues, "At the same time, many are also disconnecting from a broad range of social, community, and religious groups."[5] He expresses growing concern that while we still take time for our immediate family and distant relatives, our broad participation with social and community groups is rapidly declining. This is, in part, because of our increasingly divisive political and cultural views.[6] Henry Gass's article from the *Christian Science Monitor* provides additional constructive articles about divided communities all over the United States that are creating a range of **innovative** ways to work together for the common good.

Innovative Response: Creating Communities of Hospitality

Here is a heartwarming example of some Presbyterians in Texas that created a way to be God's offering of hospitality in a very divided situation at the border.

Several years ago, Dick Powell, the head of the Presbyterian Mo-Ranch Camp in North Texas, asked a few pastors near the southern border, "Why don't your young people ever come to our camp?" The answer stunned him: "Border security." Undocumented residents did not want to risk passing a checkpoint anywhere near the border. Dick Powell responded, "As a Christian, we believe everyone—everyone—is a child of God and created in God's image."[7]

Since it wasn't possible for these high school students

5.   Marc Dunkelman, *The Vanishing Neighbor: The Transformation of American Community* (New York: W. W. Norton, 2014), 14.

6.   Henry Gass, "Once a Nation of Joiners, Americans Are Now Suspicious of Those Who Join," *Christian Science Monitor*, January 9, 2019.

7.   Manny Fernandez, "A Summer Camp That Doesn't Care Where You Are From," *New York Times*, August 18, 2019.

living on the border to come five hours north to the 500-acre Mo-Ranch, located north of San Antonio, Dick and his team created an alternative. They designed an **innovative** way to bring their camping program to these teens. They leased a twenty-three-acre retreat situated near the border.

This weeklong camp costs Mo-Ranch $51,000. They raised the money from the hospitality of Presbyterian donors all over the state, who welcomed the opportunity to reach out to these teens. This enabled Mo-Ranch to offer this new camping opportunity to these young people for only twenty-five dollars for an entire week of camp.

Powell and his team created a new program to not only extending welcoming hospitality to these young people, but also to enable these young people and their families to navigate these very divisive times. They also helped these young campers to start exploring a broader range of options for their future after high school.

These Presbyterians designed a creative camping experience focusing on new relationships, spiritual growth opportunities, and future possibilities. An important requirement for attendance is that campers were asked to leave their phones home for the week in order to focus on one another and what they were learning.

"Vanessa, 17, said she often heard helicopters overhead—'I live right next to the border.' This was her third Mo-Ranch. 'Patience,' Vanessa said, 'is the one thing I have learned this summer. I have learned to forgive people even though they give me the hardest time. I just can't hate anymore because this camp has taught me so much.'"[8]

---

8.   Fernandez, "A Summer Camp."

"The camp helped Isaac, 16, in many ways, with the spiritual energy, the friendships, the affirmation and confidence it takes to become a dentist. Clara, 17, dreams of becoming a surgical nurse. She said she felt the stigma associated with growing up on the border . . . 'You are probably not going to go to college. You are probably not going to make it. You have to keep moving forward . . . I am going to be someone in life.'"[9]

At a worship service on the final night, campers and counselors gathered to pray, sing, and share how they planned to move forward with their dreams in times like these as they headed back home to life near the border.

Creating Innovative Opportunity for the Excluded to Share Their Story

One of the most powerful ways to bring reconciliation in these divided times is to provide creative opportunities for our invisible neighbors to share their stories. That is exactly the remarkable achievement Ladj Ly has accomplished in crafting the newest version of *Les Misérables*: "As the new *Les Misérables* opens, France has just won the World Cup and an ecstatic group of black teenagers is making its way into central Paris. The streets are flooded with people from all backgrounds draped in the colors of the French flag. This is the France the country's politicians love to idealize—a country where people of all classes, colors and religions can feel united under a common French *fierté* [pride]."

But then the scene shifts to the dreary working-class suburb of Montfermeil. It's a place plagued by police violence, ethnic clashes, and little opportunity. Lined with high-rise

9.   Fernandez, "A Summer Camp."

housing projects, factories, and dingy kebab shops, it looks nothing like the Paris audiences are used to seeing on the screen.

"The film is about the daily misery shared by everyone in Montfermeil," Ly says. And he means everyone—from the inhabitants of the graffitied high-rises to the cops who patrol them. The story follows a day in the life of Montfermeil's anti–street crime unit. After trying to arrest one teen, the unit is confronted by some of the same kids we saw celebrating France's World Cup victory in the first scene—only this time, they are throwing stones.

Many of these scenes are taken directly from the pages of Ly's own life. His family arrived in France after emigrating from Mali in the 1980s. He was raised in Montfermeil, and still lives there today. Ly is providing students such as Mbathio Beye, originally from Senegal, with opportunities they never thought they'd have. Beye says it feels like Ly opened a window: "You know, when the door is not open you know you have to go through the window? This is what he did . . . and now the door is open you can go get in."[10]

However, what has changed the most in this new film is the way it has opened the door for these struggling young refugees to tell their own stories in a way that is rare in all our societies. Mary was right: God, from generation to generation, "has performed mighty deeds with his arm; . . . he has scattered those who are proud in their inmost thoughts . . . but has lift up the humble."[11]

---

10.   Rebecca Rosman, "France Has Changed—And So Has 'Les Misérables,'" NPR, January 11, 2020.

11.   Luke 1:51–53, New International Version.

Anticipating a Growing Housing Crisis
for the Poor, the Young, and the Elderly

Now, we will shift to addressing the growing epidemic of homelessness all over our country. Housing inequities create another form of division in American society between those who have adequate or even extravagant housing and those that don't.

This new housing crisis is particularly impacting the poorest and youngest Americans. First, we are facing the greatest homeless crisis in America since the Great Recession, and cities all over America are attempting to mitigate it. According to the US Department of Housing and Urban Development's Annual Homeless Assessment Report, as of 2018, there are around 553,000 homeless people in the United States on a given night, or 0.17 percent of the population.[12]

Housing prices are increasingly beyond the reach of our neighbors and families who have marginal incomes, partly because some investors are purchasing large amounts of housing in areas that seem to be attractive to buyers. These homes are sometimes held off the market until the prices rise. This works great for the investors, but it often makes it tough for those on marginal incomes and the growing numbers of those in the middle class as well.

As a consequence, we may see a growing number of families and those without kids living in vans, cars, and tents camped alongside freeways and parks—that is, until authorities make them move. Of course, this is already happening for growing numbers of people with mental health and addiction issues.

---

12. US Department of Housing and Urban Development's Annual Homeless Assessment Report (HUD Exchange, 2018), https://tinyurl.com/y36k4z4q.

Churches and society at large are discovering new ways to live in solidarity with those on the margins in all our communities. Many are slowly learning to shift from charity to **innovative** ways to enable neighbors to become self-reliant. Here are some examples.

Community First Village

In 2013, Steven and Bethany Hubbard started a creative Catholic community as a site for homeless people in Austin, Texas. Today, this community has constructed two hundred tiny houses on twenty-seven acres. They also provide a program to enable residents to overcome difficult issues, including addiction, and help them begin the journey back to self-reliance.

Co:Here

Co:Here is one of a spectrum of less expensive rental housing options for residents of Vancouver, British Columbia. It is a unique collaboration between Grandview Church in the community, and local and provincial governments. The Co:Here Housing Community constructed twenty-six units of low-cost rental housing. It is operated by the Salisbury Community Society and is a creative example of providing low-cost housing for people with limited housing options.[13]

---

13.   Joyce Eng, "Unique Affordable Rental Housing Project Opens in Vancouver," September 3, 2018, http://coherehousing.com.

Safe Parking, LA is sponsored by the Veterans Administration. In Los Angeles, an estimated 16,500 people live in their vehicles. Keith Roads, a homeless veteran and actor, describes one of a number of safe parking lots for vets that have porta-potties: "They have food, security is good . . . I don't have to worry."[14]

Anticipating a Growing Housing Crisis for Gen Next

Most people are aware of the growing homeless crisis, but we suspect that many readers are not as aware of the growing homeless crisis for both the middle-class young and middle-class seniors who are also struggling to get by.

Recently, Tom and Christine had the opportunity to speak at an annual banquet sponsored by a campus ministry at Bloomsburg University in Pennsylvania. We were celebrating the graduation of eight students who had been active in campus ministry. This campus ministry is supported by a spectrum of mainline Protestant churches in the community. About fifty guests from the churches and a dozen students, as well as Jill, the director of campus ministry, seemed to enjoy the opportunity to get together.

When it was time for the address, Christine shared stories recalling some of her final days of medical school. When it was Tom's turn, he expressed how impressed he was by the evident enthusiastic support of these representatives from local congregations. After some introductory remarks, Tom asked them if they had any idea of how much

---

14.   www.safeparkingla.org.

debt these students were graduating with. No one offered an estimate.

Tom received permission from two of the students to share this information. The audience was stunned when he revealed that both young women were graduating with debt of over $80,000 each from this state university. Tom's single question to the audience was, "How long do you estimate it will take for these two grads to pay off their debt to begin their lives?" This audience was stunned because, like many people of older generations, most of these good people had no idea of the debt load many grads under forty are saddled with. They also had no idea how hard it will be for many middle-class young people to get started, particularly in terms of the costs of renting and buying housing.

Celebrating the Good News Generation

We are both big fans of the youth in Gen Y and Z. In fact, we will end this book celebrating Gen Next as the good news generation! They are the first internet generations. As a consequence, many are much more aware of the climate justice, racial justice, and economic justice movements than in previous times. Most importantly, a higher percentage of this demographic wants to invest their lives in serious change-making. Gen Y and Z have the opportunity to design their best lives for times like this, and they begin by exploring **innovative** new housing options that are both less expensive and more communal. We hope all who read this book will encourage Gen Y and Z to take their concerns and passion for these issues seriously. We encourage them to join other young innovators to create new ways to live and make a little difference in the world. Since many in these generations will face the dual challenges of increased school debt and rising housing prices, we encourage them to start by researching a broad range of **innovative** housing and community options. In the process, we suspect many of them could achieve a way of life more focused on joining those making an impact than on acquiring expensive housing.

A Friendly Word for the Friends and Facilitators of Gen Next

We now want to address all those who have the opportunity to work with Gen Next. First, as you know, many middle-class young are raised to expect to start their lives with a house like they grew up in, only about 20 percent nicer. College staff, youth workers, parents, and pastors who work with Gen Y and Z need to realize that this is no longer a realistic dream, particularly for those that have compelling ideas of what they want to accomplish. So, we ask all those who work with the young to encourage them to explore a broad range of ways to reduce their housing costs so they are able to more fully invest their lives addressing those issues where they want to bring real change.

Many who are part of Gen Y and Z will face higher levels of educational debt than earlier generations. As a consequence, it will not only make it difficult to qualify for housing loans, but for those that do qualify, higher college debt and higher housing costs could make their economic future much more difficult than earlier generations.

Many of them believe they are scripted to live into their parents' American dream lifestyle. Often neither they, their parents, nor even their college counselors seem to realize "that bird is not going to fly anymore." The cost of housing in many markets is simply more than many young couples can afford, particularly those that have high college debt. As a consequence, many millennials are postponing starting their families. They tell me (Tom) that it is not just the cost of housing but also the sky-high costs of childcare in many communities.

So, attempting to purchase an American dream house could be costly to personal finances and to a stable, productive future. Those making such a purchase could wind up being saddled with more school and housing debt than is manageable. The resulting large monthly payments to a mortgage company could make it impossible for them to save for their children's college costs or even have adequate resources for retirement. Finally, there is the real possibility that Social Security may not be there for Gen Next.

Imagine how these opportunities for hospitality and welcome might find creative expression in these polarized times. Imagine new ways we might create new communities that offer new forms of hospitality and reflect something of the hospitality of Jesus and that first community of believers.

Touring More Community-Based, Less Expensive Options

Those interested in alternative, less costly housing will find that alternatives are on the rise. Consider these examples.

The Tiny House Alternative

When he was nearing graduation with a business degree, Jenson Roll contacted Tom because he shared a mutual interest in community innovation. As Tom and Jenson got acquainted, Tom discovered that Jenson had found several men at his North Carolina church that were helping him build a tiny house to reduce their housing costs for life after college.

Tom was invited to speak at the Wild Goose Festival in June of 2016. Jenson offered to drive his nearly completed tiny house to the festival. Tom invited Jenson to join in his presentation of creating new possibilities for the future. They used his tiny house as the stage for their presentations, then Jenson offered the audience tours of his tiny house.

A recent episode of *Tiny House Nation* profiled the story of a family who was determined to provide money to make it possible for each of their three children to graduate college debt-free. The dad was a high school basketball coach. The mom worked in business. Together they had two sons and a younger daughter. When their first son was nearing graduation from high school, they sold their 3,000-square-foot house and used the profit from the sale to finance his schooling. They also bought a less expensive 2,000-square-foot house to make the finances work. Years later, when their second son was approaching college, they downsized again, moving into an even smaller house that was just over 1,000 square feet. As their daughter was approaching her high school graduation, Mom and Dad did their final downshift, to a 650-square-foot tiny home.

As *Tiny House Nation* toured the construction process of their much smaller dwelling, it was pretty clear that the dad wasn't sure this final downsizing would work for him. However, when they visited the completed structure and settled in, the couple were overjoyed. Remarkably, their tiny house design actually included Murphy beds so their adult children could still visit. Even more remarkable was witnessing how the parents reduced their own housing preferences for the sake of their adult children. That's compassionate innovation, to say the least.

As we tour an array of housing options, we will continue to ask the question: What does the good life of God look like for followers of Jesus in a world of Instagram envy? One option might look like parents stewarding their own housing differently in order to help their kids launch in times like these.

Tiny houses had arrived on the scene in the US well before 2016, but they are increasingly more commonplace today. We're even seeing 3D printing technology used for livable houses, which holds promise for further reducing construction costs. Already an Austin-based start-up called ICON says they can print a house nearly 200 hundred times faster than traditional stick construction—a house in a day. Right now, these printed homes max out at 800 square feet and are a bit on the heavy side, but imagine those possibilities in the coming decade.[15]

The 3D Printed House Alternative

More recently, ICON has started using 3D printing to construct fifty 3D concrete homes in Tabasco, Mexico, for low-income families. The houses are 500 square feet with two bedrooms and one bathroom. According to a 2015 Habitat for Humanity study, 1.6 billion people on the planet do not have safe housing. These 3D constructed homes could provide homes at a much smaller cost.[16]

15. "The Future of Human Shelter Has Arrived: Introducing the Vulcan II," ICON, accessed February 17, 2020, www.IconBuild.com.

16. Christina Zdanowicz, "The World's First 3-D-Printed Neighborhood Is

Also, 3D housing could be a welcome alternative to the growing homelessness crisis in America and other countries. It might even provide an alternative to young people launching their lives in a number of Western countries, like the United States, where they can't afford to buy any existing homes.

Creative Co-Living Alternatives

A number of young people in the UK are having an increasingly difficult time finding reasonably priced housing. Some young families who can't afford high-priced rentals are reportedly living in abandoned shipping containers. Recently, corporations that host numbers of British tech workers in their extensive co-working spaces have expanded into the new co-living market primarily for the young, but are also attracting retirees as well.

The Collective became the UK's first large-scale co-living space when it opened in 2016. "Since then," writes the BBC, "developers have submitted plans for 700 co-living units in Canary Wharf, 220 in Stratford . . . and 170 in London Bridge. . . . Some are calling the rise in co-living a reaction to the housing crisis faced by younger generations—skyrocketing housing costs and plateauing wages are making buying a home in the city [London] almost impossible."[17]

Let's look at Old Oak West, one of the oldest and most well-established co-living sites in London: "It boasts a gym, bar, restaurant, cinema room, roof terrace, spa, and communal lounge. It includes a small twelve-meter 'studio'

Being Built in Mexico for Families Living on 3 Dollars a Day," CNN, December 12, 2019, https://tinyurl.com/ssotscy.

17.   Winnie Agbonlahor, "Co-Living in London: Friendship, Fines and Frustration," BBC News, London, April 24, 2018, https://tinyurl.com/t8xjwwm.

room for 1,300 pounds per month, which millennials see as a good value, given all the amenities."[18]

As you can imagine, co-living has come across the pond to the United States. Innovators have discovered a fertile market among the young in the housing markets in New York and Washington, DC. Forbes reports that in the United States, "co-living is as increasingly popular as co-working, especially among millennials. They seem to be attracted by both the lower costs and the increased opportunity for community. . . . Most co-living apartments are cheaper in terms of absolute dollars, offer more flexible terms than standard leases, and provide a sense of community with almost no commitment."[19]

Co-Living for All of Life: A Design Opportunity

Remember in the last chapter, we suggested that following Jesus was more than a devotional add-on to our real lives? Following Jesus can be thought of as a design opportunity to create both a lifestyle and a time-style that reflects the way of Jesus. We encouraged you to consider joining those who are leading a way of life that is less stressed and more festive, where we take time to be present to both God and our neighbor.

Now, we want to invite you to consider two new possibilities in creating your best life with others to help you ride the waves of change in the 2020s. We particularly want you to learn to view all of life as a design opportunity. We want to show you ways of joining with others in creating Christian co-housing models that increase community and

---

18.   Agbonlahor, "Co-Living in London."

19.   Jeffrey Steele, "Is Co-Living the New Co-Working?," *Forbes*, February 7, 2019, https://tinyurl.com/rjbshcs.

reduce costs, regardless of whether you are under forty or post-fifty.

Co-Living Creativity at Goshen College

As Tom has had the opportunity to address students at Christian colleges and seminaries, he always requests to host thirty to forty students in a futures/creativity workshop, in which he invites them to create some new possibilities for life after college. Then he asks two or three of the students to share some of their most creative ideas in the final chapel presentation.

For example, Tom was asked to speak at Goshen College eight years ago. He immediately accepted because he has always been impressed by the quality of their academic offerings and their care for their students. As usual, he offered a Futures Creative Workshop for upper-division students. On this particular occasion, the workshop title was "Is There Life After Goshen?" In his first chapel session, he sketched some of the new opportunities and challenges awaiting students in the next five to ten years. Then, in the second chapel, he had four of the creativity groups from the Futures Innovation workshop the day before share some of their creative ideas for their life after Goshen. Every time he offers this two-session presentation at Christian colleges, not surprisingly, the students are much more engaged when their own classmates are up front sharing their **innovative** plans for life after college.

All four of the student groups that presented their **innovative** ideas for Life After Goshen had very engaging conversations with their fellow students right in front of the stage in the chapel. One group in particular, Brad, Brent, and Mike, seemed to stir the most student interest as they shared their dream for life after Goshen. Brent had already landed a tech job at a firm in Chicago. Brad and Mike had a dream to move to Chicago to work with an at-risk high school they knew about. They already had contacts at the high school. The three of them had already connected with a campus ministry there too. Based on what they learned about the high school and the neighborhood where it was located, they developed a plan of how they were going to work with at-risk students there. However, they had little idea of how to deal with the practical issues of getting situated in that neighborhood.

Brad shared the news that he had already started the search for an affordable rental in Chicago. During their creativity time, the three of them came up with a plan to rent a three-bedroom house together. Brad was also excited about their plan to work with at-risk students and offered to pay half the rent on a three-bedroom house to make it happen. Apart from the satisfaction of the three friends sharing their life together in Chicago, the reduced rental costs from a shared living situation would enable each of them to pay off their school debt a little quicker (which was significantly less than today).

As Tom has spoken at a number of Christian colleges over the past two decades, he has observed colleges building more expensive dormitories and expanding dining options, often with four to six food courts, to serve students. These more costly housing and dining options contribute significantly to rising school costs and student debt.

Tom's proposal was that Goshen consider creating a new intergenerational living option for students, some faculty and staff, plus some retired Mennonites. Instead of expensive dormitories and a half-dozen food courts, this shared-living model would be an intergenerational option where students and other residents would prepare meals together and perhaps even garden together. This model would be less expensive while offering an intergenerational living and learning opportunity. Like many creative ideas, this one was not adopted because it seemed not to be practical at that time.

Co-Living: A Design Opportunity for Many of Us

Over the past few years, the Pew Research Center has noted an intriguing trend in housing: people are opting to live together. In fact, since the last recession in 2007 to 2009, there has been a significant increase in the construction of intergenerational housing for white families to reduce housing costs. The major form of co-housing in the US today is imported from Denmark, where it originated in the 1960s.[20]

One of Tom's lifelong collaborators was his late friend and architect Leroy Troyer. Leroy designed a model of co-housing for one of Tom's early books. Leroy has recently gone on to his reward, but his legacy lives on for Tom and many others in the Mennonite community. Today we would encourage compassionate and creative architects to start collaborating with a new generation of Gen Y and Z to enable them to create a new range of co-communities that increase hospitality and empowerment in their neighborhoods while reducing costs. We need to challenge Christians of all generations to discover that following Jesus in the turbulent 2020s is really an opportunity to create our best lives and to join those who are creating some of the most **innovative** forms of community and hospitality.

---

20. Kelsey Campbell-Dollaghan, "The Future of Housing Looks Nothing Like Today's," Fast Company, May 6, 2019, https://tinyurl.com/y3vvelfu.

Tom recently visited a Christian co-housing unit in Grand Rapids near Calvin College, where a number of Calvin grads live. Our friends Barb and Rick Buckham also run a co-housing community called Meadow Wood on Bainbridge Island, Washington, that is a bit less expensive than some. Tom has promoted this model of co-living in his writing and speaking for over three decades.

Co-Living in Seattle to Increase Community and Reduce Costs

Before we take you on a tour of housing alternatives for the 2020s, Christine, Tom, and their Golden Retriever, Goldie, also welcome young people who are just getting started into a co-living opportunity in their home at reduced rental rates. Everyone helps out around the house and the garden, and it is a modest experience of what it is like to live in an intergenerational community. They call their home the Mustard Seed House. Over twenty years ago, they purchased a large home in Seattle when real estate was still inexpensive. They selected this spacious, ancient house because it was already divided into three distinct flats, which works great for housing an intergenerational community. The community shares a meal together once a week with a time of reflection and getting caught up with each other. In this way, they share an experience of how everyone is doing in their life and faith journey.

Tom and Christine love doing hospitality. Tom particularly enjoys cooking food from all over the world for friends from all over the world. Most have survived. Given the growing housing challenges facing many in Gen Next, Tom and Christine are encouraging people of faith to consider intergenerational living. They suspect others will also discover that it is a more mutually supportive way of life in these increasingly uncertain times. They find that young people enjoy the increased hospitality and welcome the reduced costs.

Minneapolis Leading in Creating Co-Housing for Low-Income and Recent Grads

Minneapolis is one of the first cities to embark on creating an expanded range of new modes of rental coliving, including triplexes, for both those with low incomes and students with high college debt. The city is changing codes to build less expensive multiplex cohousing including modular factory-based construction. Other regions in the United States are also expanding housing options to address the needs of low-income families and members of Gen Next who are struggling with higher school debt. For example, Oregon has just passed an ordinance to "effectively end single-family zoning starting in 2021."[21]

Consider Creating Your Own Co-Living Alternative to Increase Community and Reduce Costs

For example, some young couples starting out might welcome living in a two-bedroom, one-bath unit with shared kitchen and hospitality areas in order to reduce their housing costs. A senior in the same co-community might be satisfied with a one-bedroom, one-bath unit and share a

---

21.   Mark Trumbull, "Beyond the Picket Fence: How One City Is Creating More Affordable Housing," *Christian Science Monitor*, February 3, 2020, https://tinyurl.com/uhyro29.

kitchen and community area like some of the British models we described earlier.

The Changing Profile of Ways to Provide Support for Seniors

"Racing Towards New Possibilities" was the title of Tom's address at the 2012 gathering of the Mennonite Health Assembly in Louisville. Tom feels indebted to the Mennonites for all they have taught him about what it means to be a follower of Jesus. The Mennonite Health Association is responsible for oversight of Mennonite retirement facilities. As a result of having the opportunity over several decades to work with Mennonite churches and organizations, he shared the news that a growing number of aging Mennonites could no longer afford to live in Mennonite retirement facilities. Then, he shared a less expensive alternative that a group of older Mennonites had created in Lancaster, Pennsylvania.

This group of Mennonites created a very **innovative** mutual care network for the over fifty-year-olds, which offered hospitality and a mutual care "village" named Lancaster Downtowners.

On their website, they describe themselves as "a network of people who share a common passion for downtown Lancaster as the community of choice for their senior years. Downtowners includes individuals who have already retired and are living in the city, others who anticipate living downtown for their senior years, and younger people supportive of the Downtowners' initiative."[22] Essentially, this community of both working and retired seniors has

---

22.   www.Lancasterdowntowners.org.

created a network of mutual care. However, as you can see from the list below, they are also very active in their community.

Their shared practices include:

· An intentional retirement lifestyle connected to Lancaster City Community

· Contributing to the vitality of the city through work, volunteerism, civic leadership, and economic investment

· Personal development that nurtures the mind, body, and spirit and promotes peacemaking and right relationships with community and the environment

· Aging in place with an intergenerational community[23]

Considering Creating Intergenerational Communities for the 2020s and Beyond

After the 2007–2009 recession, architects started designing and building intergenerational housing for middle-class families again. This model can both reduce costs and increase community. Given not only the rising housing costs in the 2020s but also the growing turbulence in our society, we suspect that many would value the sense of hospitality and mutual support that Lancaster Downtowners provides.

Such models offer creative opportunities for people who are committed to the way of Jesus to create a range of new intergenerational community living experiments. It would be relatively easy to design less expensive and more cooperative living situations.

---

23. www.Lancasterdowntowners.org.

We would also be able to offer more hospitality and have more festive parties and celebrations of life offered for the purpose of inviting people to create new ways to offer community and hospitality in our divided communities. The Hutterites, the Simple Way Community, and other Christian communities would be glad to share how they do intergenerational communities that offer generous hospitality in these deeply divided times.

Reflecting on Jesus's Hospitality on the Beach

We started by **reflecting** on the radical hospitality of God, not only creating a new community but calling us all to work for a more just society. We end with an image of the risen Jesus offering breakfast on the beach to his friends, which reminds us of God's great homecoming feast where God has promised to make all things new.

Another of our favorite images of the hospitality of Jesus is found in John 21, where we encounter the risen Jesus offering breakfast to his surprised disciples. The Johannine community writes, "Early in the morning Jesus stood on the shore, but his disciples did not recognize that it was Jesus. Jesus called out to them, 'Friends, haven't you any fish?'" Initially they did not recognize Jesus. It wasn't until he instructed them to try fishing on the other side of their boat that they caught a generous number.

"When they landed they saw a fire of burning coals with fish on it, and some bread . . . Jesus said to them, come have breakfast. None of the disciples asked him, 'Who are you?' They knew it was the Lord. Jesus took the bread and gave it to them and he did the same with the fish."[24]

---

24.   John 21:4–13, New International Version.

Now picture yourself in a boat with friends or family, tired from a hard morning's work, approaching that beach. Though it's early, you and your companions are worn out, hungry, and thirsty. You see a figure calling out to you and your companions to come and join him for breakfast on the beach. As you approach, you see the fire and the freshly grilled fish, and you and your companions receive a warm welcome from this surprising beach-side chef. As you sit down to this gracious breakfast, you discover you are not alone. Jesus has set out a spread for you and so many others.

Suddenly you remember the imagery of the great homecoming feast of God in Isaiah 25:6–9:

> On this mountain the Lord Almighty will prepare a feast of rich food for all people, a banquet of aged wine—the best of meat and the finest of wines. On this mountain he will destroy the shroud that enfolds all peoples, the sheet that covers all nations. He will swallow up death forever. The sovereign Lord will wipe away the tears from all faces, he will remove the disgrace of his people from all the earth.[25]

Is it possible that the impromptu breakfast on the beach, with those first disciples, a meal that was generously prepared by the risen Jesus, was a foretaste of the great homecoming feast of God? In the next chapter, we will show how that earliest community of followers of Jesus took the hospitality of Jesus very seriously.

Before we pivot to the vital practice of innovating our best communities, reflect again. Hold these two images of God's hospitality and welcome. Imagine new ways you and those in your community might create or participate in

---

25. Isaiah 25:6–9, New International Version.

offering fresh forms of hospitality that reflect the hospitality of Jesus and his first community of followers.

Prayer

O Perfect Community,

You created the place we call home and love it. All our neighbors reflect your image. Every blade of grass, the air we breathe, the soil we till, the birds of the air, fish of the sea, and the animals of the land are a living testament to your goodness, abundance, and love. We live in communion with all this rich diversity of creation. All that is is reflective of your diversity and your unity. Your unity defines our love's aspiration. Your diversity invites us to stand in awe of the other. Help us, O God, to innovate for community together. Amen.

For Group Discussion

1. Could you imagine being part of a diverse community of neighbors, like Dwight and Lynette, who started restoring their neighborhood in Lake Hills? What are some areas in neighborhoods where you live that might welcome some community restoration activities?

2. What are some new challenges and opportunities that are likely to face your neighbors and neighborhoods in the next five to ten years? What are **innovative** ways that people of faith and churches could join others in responding?

3. Were you impressed at how biblical the value of hospitality was so central to the life and ministry

of Jesus? Were you also impressed by the radically inclusive hospitality of that first-century church?

4. Could you imagine creating a new expression of hospitality in your community that was as compassionate and creative as the example of the Presbyterian camping hospitality from Texas that we described?

5. Clearly, one of the most urgent new challenges facing our communities as we race into the 2020s is a growing housing crisis not only for the homeless, the elderly, and those on low incomes, but for young people as well. What are **innovative** new ways your church or nonprofits might repurpose the growing number of available church properties to provide low-income housing?

6. Would it be possible for leaders in your churches and nonprofits to also research the possibility of working with those creating less expensive cohousing or intergenerational housing for both the young and the elderly?

7. Could leaders in our Christian colleges and campus ministry organizations enable the students they work with to explore a much broader range of housing options to reduce their costs and free up more time to invest in their families, but also in making an impact in their communities?

8. Finally, could our churches reach out to a broad range of diverse groups in our neighborhoods to create inclusive celebrations like Dwight and Lynette's Lake Hill community?

Resources

Christine D. Pohl, *Living into Community: Cultivating Practices That Sustain Us* (Grand Rapids: Eerdmans, 2011).

Christine D. Pohl, *Making Room: Recovering Hospitality as a Christian Tradition* (Grand Rapids: Eerdmans, 1999).

Radha Agrawal, *Belong: Find Your People, Create Community, and Live a More Connected Life* (New York: Workman, 2018).

Mae Lisa Cannon, *Beyond Hashtag Activism: Comprehensive Justice in a Complicated Age* (Downers Grove, IL: InterVarsity Press, 2020).

Peter Block, *Community: The Structure of Belonging* (San Francisco: Berrett-Koehler, 2008).

John McKnight and Peter Block, *The Abundant Community: Awakening the Power of Families and Neighborhoods* (San Francisco: Berrett-Koehler, 2012).

Margaret J. Wheatley, *Who Do We Choose to Be? Facing Reality, Claiming Leadership, Restoring Sanity* (San Francisco: Berrett-Koehler, 2017).

6

Innovating in Place

*As a jazz musician, you have individual power to create the sound.
You also have a responsibility to function in
the context of other people who have that power also.*

—Wynton Marsalis

Innovating in a Hot Tub

Can we all agree that inspiration sometimes comes at odd moments? For some it's in the shower. Others, the bus. Sometimes it comes to you in a dream. We pick up this story in a hot tub in Washington state's Sudden Valley.

It's very late. The stars shine brightly through a small clearing in the towering cedars and pines of the Pacific Northwest. A small group of change-making friends have descended on a little cabin in the woods to dream, scheme, and encourage each other's opening to discover what God might be inviting each person to be and do.

Howard Lawrence and his son were among the hot tubbers that autumn night in 2013. Howard had recently resigned as the pastor of Highland Baptist Church in Edmonton, Alberta, in order to focus his time, imagination, and energy connecting and empowering his Highland neighborhood.

As Howard began by expressing his growing concern for how disconnected from one another many of his neighbors appeared to be. Eventually, he began to imagine how life might be different if even the people living on the same street could find a way to reconnect or connect for the first time. He risked sharing with the other hot tubbers his desire. He wanted to discover a means to help his neighbors get to know each other in meaningful ways. He voiced concern about the fast-paced culture of consumerism and fear. It felt to him as though it was becoming more challenging for his neighbors to get to know those living just next door. Ideas began to flow.

Howard sensed that the kind of deep changes his neighborhood needed could only emerge if the residents found new ways to collaborate together. He heard himself articulating what he had been feeling for a while, that the Holy Spirit was daring him to venture out, to try something new. It's remarkable what can happen when people candidly share their shalomic hopes with each another.

Over the following months Howard kept taking small risks, trying little experiments, and having conversations with neighbors. Looking back, he'd say that the first phase was building a stronger social fabric on each block in his neighborhood. He did this by finding one person on each block in the neighborhood to become a conversation starter for that block. Often, the conversation starter was the person or family most likely to host a party, throw a barbecue, and invite others over.

Howard encouraged these hosts to get their neighbors together and have a conversation about life together on the block: What was great? Why did they love their block? What were the growing concerns or red flags on the horizon? How might they be even more welcoming? What kinds of strengths did they bring to each other? Together, as connected people, they began sharing their hopes and dreams for the place they inhabit, and as a collective. And neighbors began to find new ways to work together for local change. Today those hosts are called "Block Connectors," and Howard's hot tub dream has become a thing of change-making beauty.

Celebrating an Abundant Community in Edmonton

Some months after their hot tub conversation Dwight learned that Howard had not only successfully facilitated some of his neighbors to connect more meaningfully, but some were themselves already starting to create new ways to make a difference in their neighborhood. Over time, Edmonton's city officials began to notice a different kind of community engagement originating from the Highland neighborhood. And the city liked what it saw.

Eventually the city of Edmonton actually hired Howard to head up an Abundant Community Initiative for all the neighborhoods in the city. Howard has developed friendships with Asset-Based Community Developers gurus John

McKnight and Peter Block,[1] and he is increasingly sought out by other cities looking to deepen the collective sense of belonging among their residents. He is a wise and thoughtful person with a profound belief in the transformative power of innovating in place.

Innovating in place always starts with a person like Howard, someone who can see a real challenge and yet discern God's invitation through that challenge and turn the challenge into a design opportunity.

Change-makers listen to their frustration with the status quo; they have a sense that another way might be possible, and they believe that if neighbors work together, with God's good help, they can do even more together than they ever alone could imagine. Our hunch is that you are a lot like Howard.

Innovation for Neighborhood Change-Making in the 2020s

In the last chapter, we focused on growing divisiveness in our cities, our communities, and even our congregations. In response, we shared some **innovative** ways people were seeking to address this divisiveness. We also discussed a growing housing crisis that is impacting a growing population of homeless, a growing number of our young who are launching their lives, and our seniors struggling to find affordable housing and community support for this period of life.

In this chapter we are narrowing our attention on innovating in place, right where you are. You don't need to move

---

1. John McKnight and Peter Block, *The Abundant Community: Awakening the Power of Families and Neighborhoods* (San Francisco: Berrett-Koehler, 2012).

somewhere or find a different group to be part of, because God's invitation to follow begins right where you are. So . . . where are you? Are you living on a farm in a rural community? If so, you can innovate in place. Are you living on the sixth floor of an apartment in the city? If so, you can innovate in place. Are you living in a mid-century ranch house in the suburbs? If so, you can innovate in place. Wherever you are *is* your starting place.

That is at least part of the meaning of Christ's call to love your neighbor. Wherever and whoever you are in proximity to here and now is where we find God's invitation to be present and to love. Starting here and now could well be the beginning of a journey that takes you to there and then—but it starts here and now.

Howard didn't start with some grand vision of saving his city. Rather, he sensed through his bodily and located experience that his neighbors felt lonely, disconnected, and powerless to affect the very place they inhabited together. Maybe he felt that a bit, too. He didn't turn away. He reflected with resurrection hope into the reality of the situation and didn't surrender to cynicism, despair, or powerlessness; he listened for what he could do amidst the fragmenting social structures of Highland.

Anticipating Neighborhood Opportunities

Throughout this book we've introduced you and your group to a lot of possible and probable changes coming your way. For example, people might debate whether climate change is real or what impact human action has on global weather patterns, but those debates become largely irrelevant in real places like Ellicott City, Maryland, which recently experienced two "1,000-year floods" within twenty-two months.

The reality of place has a profound way of transforming issues from abstraction into the real.

Look closely at your neighborhood and you will see most, if not all, of the accelerating changes that we have been talking about. It's all happening in your backyard. Human trafficking, racism, patriarchy, ableism, the prison industrial complex, climate change, classism, the housing crisis, xenophobia, gender discrimination, the mental health crisis, pollution, homophobia, rising debt levels, etc. are already in your neighborhood. They are lived realities.

The realities so physically proximate do not let a person off the hook in the same way that the ease of a theoretically debated issue does. Proximity carries responsibility. Michelle Ferrigno Warren writes, "As Christians we must not simply settle for awareness of the broken people on roads far away. Instead, we as the church must move together toward a proximate, informed response that moves toward the alleviation of injustice."[2]

An abstract conversation about the "signs of coming change" invites debate, often resulting in disagreement and inaction. A person can imagine an op-ed in the *New York Times* about a "coming crisis," or a person can picture a reporter on CNN graphing global trends on their news app and see them as quite theoretical.

Do you know what grounds all these things in the real world? Place, or more specifically, *your* place. When your home or workplace floods, when brush fires force you to evacuate, when your identity gets stolen, when you can no longer afford housing in the neighborhood you've called home—these events speak to the truth that place is grounding for us all. **Anticipating** changes that may impact our

2.   Michelle Ferrigno Warren, *The Power of Proximity: Moving Beyond Awareness to Action* (Downers Grove, IL: InterVarsity Press, 2017), 16.

place and **reflecting** on the impact of those changes are important precursors to creating **innovative** responses *before* the waves of change fully arrive.

Anticipation in Place

The vital three-step dance must begin by enabling leaders in a neighborhood to **anticipate** new opportunities and challenges that are likely to impact the lives of people in their neighborhood in the next five to ten years. These changes may range from rising property values, to new economic opportunities on the horizon, to reinventing local high schools so that students can focus their final two years developing a competency in coding, or apprenticing with an electrician, or earning a certificate in game design.

It begins when you and your group make the shift from intellectually attending to the vast array of possible global changes to actually attending to the realities that are likely to impact your neighborhood. Innovating in place is the ground for seeing and feeling the impact of your actions. We want to offer you and your group a glimpse into how you might anticipate a trend that you foresee coming your way and position yourself to transform it into actionable innovation.

Reflecting in Place . . . What Is Our Calling?

An important question we need to reflect on as we continue this conversation on innovating in place is the same question asked of Jesus, which prompted his telling of the Parable of the Good Samaritan: "Who is my neighbor?" We are going to start by inviting you to reflect on what Jesus says life is all about. If you are committed to following in the Jesus Way, what do you think you've committed to? It's a fundamental question.

Robert Lupton, a leader in urban ministry, was invited to speak at Urban Emphasis Week at a conservative Christian college known for its high view of scripture. During one lively discussion Lupton asked the students, "What is the number one mandate for Christians?"[3]

"Evangelize!" was the emphatic response.

Lupton pressed them a little harder, "What did Christ say was the top priority for his followers?"

"Make disciples," they responded with some confidence.

Lupton responded, "I know that evangelizing and making disciples is important," he agreed, "but what did Christ actually say was the most important mandate for his followers?"

After a moment or two of reflective silence, a student at the back of the room ventured a hesitant response. "You mean 'thou shalt love the Lord thy God with all thy soul and all thy mind and the second is like unto it. Thou shall love thy neighbor as thyself.'"

"Absolutely," Lupton agreed, "that's exactly what our Lord said . . . I'm wondering if you have any classes here in the college on loving your neighbor? I know you have an entire department of evangelism. Who teaches Neighboring 101?"[4]

Lupton's question is intriguing. Why have evangelism,

---

3. Robert Lupton has invested his life living in, learning from, and innovating in place. Lupton is the founder of FCS (Focused Community Strategies) Urban Ministry in Atlanta and has authored numerous important books on urban neighborhoods, including *Toxic Charity: How Churches and Charities Hurt Those They Help (and How to Reverse It)* and *Theirs Is the Kingdom: Celebrating the Gospel in Urban America*.

4. Robert Lupton, "Neighboring 101," https://fcsministries.org, September 10, 2019.

discipleship, or even peacemaking and social justice often been given the place of priority in Christian circles, with so much less emphasis placed on learning and developing practices, postures, and the narrative placing love of God and neighbor as the primary focus of Jesus's Way of discipleship? Jesus was very clear about what life is all about. Loving relationships. Love God and love your neighbor as yourself. And this is precisely why we want to begin this chapter in a more reflective space. This chapter is all about innovating in place.

Reflecting in Place: Loving God and Loving Neighbor

Sometimes in the Western world it almost feels like communicating gratitude is becoming a countercultural act. Diana Butler Bass, in *Grateful: The Transformative Power of Giving Thanks*, notes that "in 2014 Pew Research found that 78% of US adults reported feeling grateful on a regular basis. In 2016 Pew found the electorate was angrier and more fearful, and more divided than ever."[5] She went on to write, "I set out to look for ways to peer under the layers and find something everyone can celebrate." Along the way, writing in her gratitude journal and interviewing people far and wide, Bass discovered unexpected blessings. Since the 2016 election, she says, "We have begun asking each other what really matters. We have begun more honest self-reflection. We are examining our mutual love of democracy, our mutual ideas about what is unacceptable. People

---

5. "Diana Butler Bass: Gratitude isn't just an emotion," Faith & Leadership, May 29, 2018, https://tinyurl.com/vth6ezr.

are examining their own traditions, rediscovering ethical lines and finding friends among their enemies."[6]

Bass states that she too takes a seat at the gratitude table, "where people celebrate abundance, serve one another, and make sure all are fed. People give with no expectation of return, and joy replaces obligation. This vision of gratitude is truly virtuous, sustains the common good, ensures a circle of equality, and strengthens community."[7]

Bass recognizes the Western cultural view of gratitude as "a structure of debt and duty." Imagine a benefactor giving us a gift. "We are the beneficiaries of that gift, and we are in debt. . . . I owe you a debt of gratitude." Bass contrasts the "debt and duty" structure with Jesus's advice about hosting a dinner party. Jesus suggests that instead of inviting your family, friends, and your wealthy neighbors to your party, "invite the poor, the crippled, and all those people who can never repay you."[8] Here, Jesus undercuts the whole idea of "debt and duty."

God invites you and your group in the particularity of your place to follow Jesus into the practice of a more radical form of inclusion where you open up to receive others, especially those you in your particular context might assume have nothing to offer. You just might be surprised!

Reflecting on Gratitude for Your Place

As you and your group come to know your place even more fully, you will see some things that you wish were different. You will see suffering and pain in ways you may have driven

---

6. Cathy Lynn Grossman, "Be Thankful, Save the World?," *Sojourners*, July 2018, 38.

7. Grossman, "Be Thankful, Save the World?," 41.

8. Luke 14:13.

past or overlooked, but you will also become more grateful. Your neighborhood is amazing, and it is filled with glorious creatures, great and small. Fan those seeds of gratitude into flames until your heart is filled with the warmth of appreciation for God's generosity.

Jonah Goldberg writes, "Gratitude is the opposite of entitlement and resentment. Gratitude says, 'you didn't have to do this and I am appreciative that you did.' It can be a difficult thing to maintain."[9]

Becoming more grateful is key to helping us all receive our place and its residents with greater openness. Wouldn't we have a much better possibility of working together, in all our communities, if we expressed our gratitude? Gratitude does not erase or minimize the very real concerns, fears, or injustices present within our contexts, but it frames the conversation differently.

Reflecting on Recovering Gratitude and Compassion in Your Neighborhood

Historically, the word *parish* was used to describe a church's relationship to their neighbors and neighborhood. It tended to view neighborhoods though the lens of God's shalomic imagination. Yet today many people hear the word *parish* and think of a church's building rather than the place in which a church is located. The parish church existed to love God by learning to love its neighbors.

Over time, as modern churches placed greater emphasis on shared beliefs, interpretations, worship styles, denominational distinctives, and property management, the mission began to resemble marketing or franchising more

---

9.   Grossman, "Be Thankful, Save the World?," 39.

than a rooted sense of love of neighbor. In fact, a surprising number of churches often have very little connection with the communities where they are planted.

Reflecting in Place

Tragically, the Christian tradition is replete with examples of well-meaning people who started missionally innovating without carefully **reflecting** on the place where they were planted. When that happens, the powerful tend to unknowingly project foreign values and colonize the less powerful. People sometimes report feeling violated. We know leaders and their Christian communities want something better for the place and people you call home. However, it is essential that we consider joining those churches that take the time to reflect, with their neighbors in the community, on what the "best" does look like. It is essential that you and your group learn to listen to where you are. To lovingly innovate in place, you would be wise to intentionally do three interrelated things: get to know your place, foster gratitude for your place, and open yourself up to love your place.

Knowing Your Place

You are not everywhere. You are somewhere. You may have moved many times or lived on the same plot of land your whole life. You are somewhere right now. There is a place you call home. Your place is God's gift to you and those who share it with you. Your place is your teacher. Your place doesn't force itself on you; it is the kind of teacher that whispers to you. It invites you to slow down and listen. It woos you to mindful attention to the impact of your footprints. It bids you to notice and seek communion with all its inhabitants. Place is the platform to discover the real. The primary thing place teaches, if we will listen, is faithful presence.

As Fyodor Dostoyevsky once wrote, "One cannot love what one does not know."[10] Getting to know place is vital to following in the way of Jesus. Go for walks in the neighborhood, learn its histories, observe who holds power and who is silenced, who are its heroes and villains. What is the watershed saying, or your soil? Who is its economy working for? And who is out in the cold? What plants and animals also inhabit your space? Who makes decisions about its built environment? Are its buildings, roadways, and utilities designed for creation and humans or for profit and efficiency? Who is already there with you? What do they see or hear from their experience of the place you're sharing together? Where do you see systemic evil, injustice, or oppression? Where do you see friendship, collaboration, signs of the Spirit, or glimpses of God's shalom?

Celebrating the Innovative Impulses of the Parish Collective

Since the publication of *The New Parish: How Neighborhood Churches Are Transforming Mission* by Paul Sparks, Tim Soerens, and Dwight in 2014, this book has given birth to a movement of churches not only waking up to their neighborhoods but learning to work with their neighbors in creating a festive array of new **innovative** neighborhoods.

Dwight and his two collaborators Paul Sparks and Tim

---

10.   Fyodor Dostoyevsky, *Demons* (1872; repr., London: Penguin Classics, 2008).

Soerens and their many friends in Britain, Australia, Canada, and the United States have helped launch a remarkable movement of neighborhood renewal in parishes throughout many different countries. With so many difficult challenges facing us, one of the most hope-filled innovations is neighbors in many different places joining hands to make a real difference in their neighborhoods.

New Parish Innovation in Action!

One of the practices in which Parish Collective often guides leaders is a mapping exercise. Part of the mapping involves identifying people, businesses, organizations, religious communities, and schools that are proactively seeking to love their neighborhood. After mapping these neighborhood allies, leaders are encouraged to spend a significant block of time connecting with some of those organizations to hear a bit of their story, to thank them for their service, and to wonder if there might be some way to bless or encourage them. That's it. Not to start something, not even to partner. But to listen, learn, thank, and encourage. There is so much good already happening. In fact, we will conclude this chapter with one example of how people working in New Parish initiatives are experiencing new levels of neighborhood engagement and change-making.

Coming to know your place and fostering gratitude for your place will open you up to loving your place.

Reflecting in Place . . . Love Your Place

In just a moment, we're going look at some beautiful examples of designing in place, and when we do you will quickly see that meaningful innovation is not simply the methodical application of new ideas. Rather, it is birthed from love. As love grows, your passion for the holistic flourishing of your place and all its inhabitants also grows. Your place is telling you where innovation needs to occur, how it needs to occur, and when.

Dietrich Bonhoeffer, in *Life Together*, famously wrote, "The person who loves their dream of community will destroy community, but the person who loves those around them will create community."[11] As you and your group continue to love your place and all its inhabitants, you are far more likely to discover God's shalomic good news.

It is vital that innovating in place emerges not out of any one person's dream for what the place could be, but as a natural expression of loving God and loving your neighbors, by loving your neighborhood. Reflect deeply on how you might come to know your place, to foster thankfulness for your place, and then to lovingly innovate in place out of hearts of gratitude for the flourishing of all. Let's pivot from **reflecting** to bringing innovation into dynamic relationship.

Innovating in Place

We want to look at three highly probable trends that will likely impact your group in the coming decade, while highlighting a few examples of groups who have chosen to

---

11. Dietrich Bonhoeffer, *Life Together* (New York: HarperCollins, 2009).

innovate in their own places. The three probable changes coming your way are climate change, the coming recession in the 2020s, and ever-mounting class divisions. Let's start by looking at innovating in place through the lens of climate change.

Anticipating the Climate Crisis

As the last decade came to a close, seventeen-year-old Greta Thunberg sailed into the global consciousness, due in part to her carbon-neutral solo voyage from Sweden to the United States to raise awareness of our accelerating climate crisis. She was already well-known in her homeland as an advocate for creation care. The prior year, she began to regularly cut classes in order stand in front of the Swedish Parliament and protest inaction in the face of the crisis. Thousands of teens eventually joined her.[12] Reportedly seven million people all over the world would eventually join in her protest. After that, she was selected by *Time* magazine as "Person of the Year."

Her speech before the United Nations General Assembly in the fall of 2019 pushed the climate conversation front and center. In her TEDx talk she said, "I was diagnosed with Asperger's syndrome, OCD, and selective mutism. That basically means I only speak when I think it's necessary. Now is one of those moments!"[13]

The 2020s could be the make-or-break decade in reversing the climate crisis. As a species on this planet, human

---

12.   Jonathan Watts, "A Teen Started a Global Climate Protest. What Are You Doing?," *Wired*, March 12, 2019, https://tinyurl.com/uo8oftc.

13.   Jeff Brady (August 28, 2019), "Teen Climate Activist Greta Thunberg Arrives in New York After Sailing the Atlantic," NPR.org. Archived from the original on October 2, 2019.

beings will either make significant changes to our practices or we will go over a tipping point, after which weather patterns, temperature, and sea levels will forever alter our existence. We already are witnessing animals, birds, and sea creatures struggling to survive amidst rising ocean temperatures, melting polar ice caps, and the recent horrific fires in Australia that killed a record number of animals. It is reported that, "Dangerous new hot zones are spreading around the world. Major parts of our world have passed two degrees Celsius of warming, a *Post* investigation found."[14] One of the major reasons this is an important warning is because we are witnessing a growing number of agricultural regions, particularly in poorer parts of world, that will no longer be arable because of these rapidly rising temperatures. After years of slowly reducing the numbers of the global poor on our small planet dying of starvation and malnutrition, we could see their numbers begin to increase again. Here are some **innovative** ways that people of faith are responding to the accelerating climate crisis.

Innovating in Place . . . Young Evangelicals for Climate Action

Young Evangelicals for Climate Action (YECA) are committed to act and advocate together. They are building a movement of young evangelicals to overcome the adverse impacts of climate change and pursue sustainable lives that reduce carbon impact.

You and your group already know the earth's climate is changing and can feel the changes in your corner of the world. Climate change presents a great—arguably the

---

14. Chris Mooney and John Muyskens, "Dangerous New Hot Zones Are Spreading around the World," *Washington Post*, September 11, 2019.

greatest—design opportunity. You are likely already taking some very important steps to recycle and reduce your carbon footprint, but we thought it might be helpful to offer just a few examples of other communities who are innovating in place for the sake of the earth.

Teaching Kids to Farm inside the City

Matt Gordon lives in the Cully neighborhood of Portland, Oregon, and is active with the people of Trinity Lutheran Church. Matt and his team came up with a creative way to make a difference in both his neighborhood and his church. They started a Young Farmers Club to teach elementary-aged children how to garden and care for God's good creation. What helped Matt to make a difference locally was his church securing a lease on a half-acre in their neighborhood. Not only are the kids learning to garden and care for our natural world, but the church enjoys the fresh produce for meals they prepare for church gatherings.[15]

Teaching Adults and Church Leaders about Earth

After years of pastoring in the Evangelical Covenant Church, James Amadon left his congregational work, sensing a profound call to follow Christ into creation care. While still finishing a doctorate at Duke University in environmental stewardship, James secured a beautiful forty-acre wooded site an hour north of Seattle. James and his board at a nonprofit called Circlewood are now actively involved in developing the property. They are building a retreat site where college students, church leaders, and

---

15.   Josh Volk, "Small Farm, Real Profit," *Christian Science Monitor*, October/November 2017, 38–42.

families with kids can come and learn how to live more sustainably in times like these. James and his growing team hope this venture will equip church leaders to start trying to help both their congregations and the neighborhoods in which they are located to become more sustainable as well. As their website states, "Circlewood is a community of people who are on this way together. Our work is focused on supporting one another and cultivating other communities that love and care for all of creation. Our work is based in the Puget Sound region of Cascadia (the Pacific Northwest), but we are part of a transformative, global movement. We are disciples—learners—who encourage and challenge one another with a lot of grace. We are rooted in the Christian tradition, but open to all who want to share in the journey."[16]

Spotlighting the Impact of Climate Change on Local Wildlife

Linda Cheung is an artist living in Miami, Florida. Cheung told a local newspaper, "Climate change is often seen by Americans as something that is impacting the rest of the world, not them, but the impact of climate change is much more salient here in Miami."[17]

Linda is part of a team of local designers and artists using what they call *Techno-Charged Art* to create a unique type of mural that does more than just beautify their neighborhoods. Each mural uses a form of augmented reality technology. "Passersby will be able to hold their phones up to any animal in the mural and see a short video using a

---

16.   www.circlewood.online.

17.   Meg O'Connor, "New Wynwood Mural Uses Augmented Reality to Spark Conversation on Climate Change," *Miami New Times*, January 15, 2019.

soon-to-be-released app called the *Anthropocene Extinction*. There will be a video for each animal in the mural featuring music and narration that tells about the sixth mass extinction event, which some scientists say is happening right now and is mainly the result of human activity."[18]

The Rich and Poor Divide in Your Neighborhood

The "income inequality in America is the highest it's been since the Census Bureau started tracking it."[19] We have a larger percentage of people living in poverty than other Western countries, with less access to health care. The expanding economic divide between rich and poor is not only widening the gulf in incomes in America. It is helping the rich live longer lives while cutting short the lives of those who are struggling, according to a study recently released by the Government Accountability Office.[20]

In nearly every culture throughout human history, economic class has been one of the great dividers of people. Although wealth has been measured differently in various cultures over the millennia, one of the great biblical shalom questions involves the relational dynamic of rich and poor. Much of the Bible revolves around this profound, heart-revealing, and faith-revealing question.

If you're hoping we might offer you and your group the definitive "right way" to transform class inequity into God's shalomic imagination, we're going to sorely disappoint you. The work is profoundly yours to do.

---

18. O'Connor, "New Wynwood Mural."

19. Taylor Telford, "Income Inequality in America Is the Highest Since the Census Bureau Started Tracking It," *Washington Post*, September 26, 2019.

20. Lola Fadulu, "Gap Between Rich and Poor Gets Bigger," *New York Times*, September 11, 2019, 15.

Within your neighborhood context you have people who are poor and you have people who are wealthy, and increasingly so in both directions. Your neighborhood is quite literally the ground where the two meet. Reciprocal relationship across the very thing that divides—in this case wealth—is part of the daring of the gospel. As the apostle Paul once communicated to the churches of Galatia, we are invited into a faith that transcends all divides: "There is neither Jew nor Gentile, neither slave nor free, nor is there male and female, for you are all one in Christ Jesus."[21] In other words, for the followers of Jesus, we are part of a movement that transcends these divides, a movement that seeks to manifest God's shalom by working with those who seek to empower the vulnerable as part of the work of justice in all of our communities.

Katja Dombrowski states:

> Despite progress in many areas such as fighting global hunger and poverty, social inequality keeps growing. It undermines social cohesion and trust in democracy, hampering economic growth and preventing social advancement. The whole of society is affected. That is true in rich and poor countries. According to Oxfam, rising disparities of income and wealth are among the biggest challenges in economic, social, and political terms.[22]

Class division is growing and making it more challenging for people to collaborate. It is essential that all people of faith seek to tear down socially constructed barriers to mutual relationships and build bridges across the economic spectrum. We thought it may be useful to highlight

---

21. Galatians 3:28, New International Version.

22. Katja Dombrowski, "Inequality: Re-distributing Money and Power," Development and Cooperation, March 25, 2017, https://tinyurl.com/sz3klrp.

just a handful of people who are working to bring change in communities that are suffering from this economic inequality.

Investing for the Shalom of God

The Sisters of St. Francis of Philadelphia set up a corporate investment portfolio in the 1980s. This order is now using their stake in these corporations to enable them—in jiu-jitsu fashion—to leverage their investor status to shape the practices of corporations in which they invest: "Led by Sister Nora Nash, the order's director of corporate responsibility, the nuns have used their dividends to provide capital and mentorship to women of color entrepreneurs and build infrastructure in developing nations." But the sisters have also lobbied airlines to combat human trafficking, gun retailers to amend their sales practices, and grocery stores and restaurants to promote healthier menu options." Sister Nora and her friends seem to maintain a broad range of innovations, which emerge from their local awareness to address class issues.[23]

Access for All

"As the pastors of University Church in a city known for its gun violence," says Rev. Julian DeShazier, "we are trying to re-write Chicago's murder narrative into a story of peace and care." Rev. DeShazier was a prime mover behind the South Side's efforts to have its own Level One adult trauma center so that gun victims don't have to be taken across the city for care. This is a profound example of how clas-

---

23. Liz Brazile and Sydney Worth, "Nuns Shaking Up the Status Quo," *YES!*, Winter 2019, 12–13.

sism and institutional racism are twisted together. More recently, he and the people of the University Church where he serves provided sanctuary to undocumented fathers.[24] Rev. DeShazier is a clarion example of a person who is innovating in place. He is listening. What is his place inviting? What are the residents of his place inviting?

Sharing New Technologies and Techniques in Uganda

Joan Nabbed's school day in Uganda is filled with reading and writing and sweet potatoes. In fact, "The seventh grader is one of 11,200 students in Uganda being trained as an evangelist for improved strains of new improved forms of sweet potatoes." The seed potato has always been an important crop in Uganda. The East African nation is the leading producer of potatoes in Africa, and second only to China in the world. The vegetable has taken on heightened significance in recent years mitigating malnutrition, food insecurity, and poverty.

Some of the new strains of sweet potatoes being developed in Uganda are ten times more nutritious than some of the other varieties. Children are not just being trained to be innovators, but they are also being prepared to educate their parents. Joan said, "I was enthusiastic to learn the new techniques of growing seed potatoes." She added, "I was also interested in any skills that would help me improve our income at home."[25]

---

24.   Julian DeShazier, "Showing Up," *Sojourners*, July 2018, 29.

25.   Christopher Bendana, "How Ugandan School Children Teach Their Parents to Prosper," *Christian Science Monitor Weekly*, December 3, 2018, 19.

A Walking School Bus in Providence

"Every weekday morning," begins one story, "Yuselly Mendoza walks the streets of Olneyville, a low income, predominately Latino neighborhood on the west side of Providence, Rhode Island. She and another woman don bright yellow jackets and set out at 8:05 from the corner of Salmon Street and Manton Avenue across the street from Sanchez Liquors and a vacant weed-choked lot. They follow a route that meanders through the neighborhood, stopping along the way to pick up school children who walk with them, before reaching the William D'Abate Elementary School. A total of thirty-five kids take *The Walking School Bus*."[26] In a shalomic world, children are safely transported from home to school and back again. Mendoza is revealing the reign of God while exposing the class inequality their neighborhoods have been experiencing.

Starting Economic Cooperatives in Communities of Need

One of the most important forms of innovation has come from the rising numbers of economic cooperatives around the world:

> In stock-owned businesses, such as those you find on Wall Street, owners can live anywhere. They never have to use the goods or services that the company offers. . . . This separated ownership can lead to a lack of concern about the impact of the business on communities. After all, the main interest of the investor is getting a financial return on investment. . . . Cooperatives are fundamentally different. Co-ops blend together the best of the free market with an ownership model

---

26. Joseph Margulies, "Communities Need Neighborhood Trusts," *Stanford Innovative Review* (Spring 2019): 48.

that requires the co-op to be responsible to the people who actually use the goods or services. The owners are the users of the business. Here in the US there are more than 39,000 cooperatives.[27]

There are four primary co-op models: producer co-ops, consumer co-ops, purchasing co-ops, and worker co-ops.

Cooperative Home Care co-op provides in-home health care for the elderly and injured. In this model the majority-Latina workers are not just employees, they are also owners. Each employee has one vote and participates in the selection of the governing board. They also live locally and therefore tend to be more responsive to the needs of a community.[28]

Jonathan Rowe, in his important book *Our Common Wealth*, states, "Unlike the market, which is organized to maximize short term private gain, the commons is (or should be) organized to preserve the shared assets of the future generations and spread their benefits more or less equally among the living."[29]

Imagine what might emerge if you and your group did an assessment of the co-ops already in existence in your neighborhood and led a mini-campaign to help neighbors benefit from such practical collaboration. It could be that after you've done your assessment you'll discover a legitimate need to initiate a new type of co-op, such as the co-op described below that was innovated in North Minneapolis.

---

27. Jonathan Rowe, *Our Common Wealth: The Hidden Economy That Makes Everything Else Work* (San Francisco: Berrett-Koehler, 2013), 5.

28. Adam Schwartz, "Creating a Cooperative Economy," PCC Community Market Sound Consumer Newsletter, May 2018, 1 and 3, https://tinyurl.com/qo6j8rx.

29. Rowe, *Our Common Wealth*, 5.

Transforming Unjust Banking into Neighbors
Supporting Neighbors

The stated goal of Village Financial is to "serve the under-served Black community of North Minneapolis, who have been preyed upon and excluded from traditional financial institutions."[30] The founder Lea Connelly, together with a group of North Minneapolis residents, had had enough of predatory payday loan companies ripping off members of their neighborhood.

They chose to turn generations of racially biased and discriminatory banking practices into a design opportunity. Together, they started their own economic cooperative with the backing of a national organization called the Financial Cooperative. Its goal is to give control of capital to their community, which has been marginalized by the economic practices largely controlled by outsiders who extracted wealth from North Minneapolis, only to put it in the pockets of the already wealthy.[31]

Celebrating the New Parish Neighborhood Creativity
in Shoreline

The last weekend of every April, the New Parish hosts the Inhabit Conference at the Seattle School of Theology and Psychology here in Seattle. If you are interested in experiencing the remarkable kind of neighborhood creativity for this decade of accelerating change, please come visit. One of the highlights every year is four or five New Parish Innovators sharing some of the remarkable change-making they

---

30.   https://villagefinancial.org.

31.   Ivy Brashear, "When You Own the Bank Down the Street," *YES!*, Winter
      2019, 35.

and their neighbors have been doing in the United States, Canada, Australia, Britain, and in non-Western nations.

One remarkable example of neighborhood change-making being done by these New Parish Innovators is Jessica Katola. Here is the story of what she and her team are birthing in a place called Shoreline, Washington.

This is the story of our journey to reimagine church in such a way that it was more than a once a week gathering but a way of life. We didn't want to just attend church but to BE the church and to embody the way of Jesus that was compelling in the everyday stuff of our lives. Frankly, we were tired of the glaring gap between the words of Jesus and our lived experience.

And so we set out to be a practicing church. We realized no magic or osmosis was going to transform us to be more like Christ but that it would take practice to follow in the way of Jesus and we needed tangible practices of formation, mission and community. We needed a transformational community in which to grow our love for God and neighbor.

And Shoreline, Washington, became the testing ground for this love. A small city of 56,000 just north of Seattle. There is much beauty and opportunity here with the Puget Sound as our border and the Aurora thoroughfare that connects us to the flow of the city. Thought of, at one time, as white affluent suburbia yet with the gentrification of Seattle proper, there has been a growing influx of diverse and immigrant population that is bringing a newfound richness here in our semi-urban context.

On this journey to reimagine church, I signed up for Leadership in the New Parish in the fall of 2012. It was a gut move and one I would not regret, and yet I had no idea how it would shape my future reality. At the time I was on staff at our small but vibrant vineyard church and director of our local nonprofit, but my paradigm for what the church could look like shifted along with my entire life. I couldn't have predicted that I would pastor a neighborhood church within the next three years.

Or is church when we show up in force for neighborhood projects? Both Ryan and Courtney, who are part of our community, serve on the Richmond Highlands neighborhood association. Just recently, we were a part of a process to create a mural in our neighborhood. It was a forgotten corner by the bus stop on Aurora, full of needles and trash. But we chose an artist and design and celebrated together as it was installed in our neighborhood with pizza and a pitcher of beer.

Or does church include the community meals we share with Turning Point children and their families, tutors, and neighbors? As we gather around the table and share our cultural dishes from Mexico, the Philippines, Eritrea, Somalia, and Pakistan, I feel like we get a taste of heaven here on earth. This is Lynn, our director, with Anna, who has experienced a lot of disruption, recently removed from her parents' home and living with her aunt and uncle. But here she is beaming as she is showcasing her art and her dreams to be a writer.

Or is it church when we gather in our local Ridgecrest Pub and discuss weighty matters of theology and salvation over a locally crafted beer? We have very few gathering spots in our neighborhood and so we do our best to frequent the ones we have—and we just love this one next to the Crest Theater. We dream about creating something similar in our Richmond Highlands neighborhood. A place where neighbors can meet and hold events and come together for the good of the neighborhood.

Or is church when we invite our neighbors out for a beautification day and pick up trash in the neighborhood? Or is it when we share meals with our Eritrean friends, Efrem and Senait? Or is it church when we gather for outdoor BBQs, fire pits and holiday parties? Or is it church when we come together with our Muslim brothers and sisters for listening events and peace feasts? Or is it church when we gather with other faith leaders in the city or show up for community task forces?

As we have reimagined church as a people rooted in the neighborhood to participate in the flourishing of this place, there is a richness and a wholeness to our lives that we have never experienced before. And so we pray that God would be revealed here in us the embodied body of Christ—as church is experienced around the table, and hopes are shared on the bus and at the coffee shop and in the community forums—we pray for heaven to meet earth as our neighbors begin to see what God is like—LOVE. For this, this is church.[32]

***

All of the above examples are organizations started by people like you and members of your church or organization who sensed that Jesus might be inviting them to a more shalomic way of life in their neighborhoods. Most of the time innovation emerges when the status quo is no longer tolerable. It might be worth exploring questions like: What doesn't work? Where is pain in your place? What systems of oppression are pleading for you to act? Where does your heart break? Your denomination, church, or nonprofit can participate in this kind of neighborhood empowerment in the place where you live and worship.

These stories represent a tiny glimpse into the many followers of Christ who are innovating in place to transform class divisions into a more shalomic way of life together. God can and does ignite our imaginations to create

---

32.   Jessica Ketola, "Reimagining Church in the Neighborhood," The Practicing Church PechaKucha.docx, Inhabit Conference, 2019.

innovative ways to both be a difference and make a difference, responding to new challenges facing us in this world of accelerating change.

The practicality of place grounds a group of people in relationship to one another. God created experience this way. All it takes to be neighbors is to share a place in common. You don't get to choose your neighbors. But you are invited to learn what it looks like to live into faithful presence with them. Innovation in place is in practical terms what it looks like to love God and express your gratitude by loving your neighbor as you love yourself.

In the next chapter we'll turn our attention to innovating as Christ's church.

Prayer

Gracious God,

When you chose to reveal yourself, you became a human being and you moved into a small fishing community around the Sea of Galilee in northern Israel. You revealed yourself, *Yeshua of Nazareth*. You were located. You identified with a real context. You were particular. A body in a place. Help us attend to the gift of our particularity. Our bodies in our places. By your Spirit help us to discover the wonder of where we are. Grow within us a deep sense of gratitude for the gift of this land, these people, and all the things that make this neighborhood *your* neighborhood. And we pray that you would give us wisdom and courage to surrender our "vision" of what we might like for our place, and instead innovate out of love for our place knowing that you already love it and call it your home. Amen.

For Group Discussion

1. Where do you see glimpses of God's shalom? How could you support the good you see?

2. Where do you see "evil" at work in your place? How can we bear witness in our life and body to God's shalom in the face of injustice?

3. Where are you? What practices or postures could you engage that might open you up to learn more about where you are, and who is already there with you?

4. Where have you seen examples of churches that are already joining others in neighborhood change-making?

5. What are some examples of new challenges that are likely to impact neighbors in this decade where you live?

6. As you reflect on Jesus's call to live with both gratitude and compassion, how might you respond to some of these new opportunities in your neighborhood?

7. How might you and your friends enlist other participants in your neighborhood in ways that make a difference, as in the New Parish example at the end of the chapter?

8. How could you create ways to celebrate every step forward with friends at church and in your neighborhood?

Resources

Paul Sparks, Tim Soerens, and Dwight J. Friesen, *The New Parish* (Downers Grove, IL: InterVarsity Press, 2014).

Samuel Wells, *A Nazareth Manifesto: Being with God* (Hoboken, NJ: Wiley, 2015).

Jay Pathak and Dave Runyon, *The Art of Neighboring: Building Genuine Relationships Right Outside Your Door* (Grand Rapids: Baker, 2012).

Howard A. Snyder, *Salvation Means Creation Healed* (Eugene, OR: Wipf & Stock, 2011).

7

Innovating as Church

You must give birth to your images.
They are the future waiting to be born.
Fear not the strangeness you feel.
The future must enter you
long before it happens.
Just wait for the birth,
For the hour of new clarity.

—Rainer Maria Rilke

A new priest named Mindar is holding forth at Kodaiji, a 400-year-old Buddhist temple in Kyoto, Japan. Like other clergy members, this priest delivers sermons and goes around the temple connecting with worshipers. But Mindar has some unusual traits. A body made of aluminum and silicone, for starters. Mindar is a robot.

Designed to look like Kannon, the Buddhist deity of mercy, the million-dollar robotic priest is an attempt to reignite people's passion for their faith in a country where religious affiliation is on the decline. For now, Mindar is not AI-powered. It just recites the same pre-programmed sermon about the Heart Sutra over and over. But the robot's creators are planning on giving it learning capabilities that will enable it to tailor feedback to worshipers' specific spiritual questions and ethical quandaries.

"This robot will never die," said Tensho Goto, the chief steward at the temple, Vox reported. "It will just keep updating itself and evolving. With [the infusion of artificial intelligence], we hope it will grow in wisdom to help people overcome even the most difficult troubles. It's changing Buddhism."[1] AI religion is upon us. Welcome to the future.

Sampling High-Tech Faith in Troubled Times

This is a daunting time to be a Christian leader. Western countries are seeing increasing numbers of churches graying and declining. While not many churches have AI pastors yet, there is a very active search for new possibilities, including using new tech. More pastors rely on online tools for liturgies, robust biblical language programs for engaging the Greek, Hebrew, and Aramaic texts, and social media to *appear* connected. We can't forget that many multisite churches simulcast their sermons. Some have even experimented with 3D holographic preachers, and today if you want to go to church, well . . . there's an app for that.

As we race into this new decade of accelerating tech, some of the megachurches in the US are leading the charge. For example, in 1996, Graig Groeschel started Life Church in a garage in Edmond, Oklahoma. Today, it is the largest church in the United States on a huge campus. Ten years

---

1.   Cheryl K. Chumley, "Robot Priests, A.I. Gods Transforming the World of Worship," *The Washington Times*, September 17, 2019, https://tinyurl.com/un5wjej.

ago, they launched an internet church, inviting visitors from all over the world. Reportedly, Life Church now has 70,000 members composed both of those that come to their campus and those who worship online.

Not surprisingly, Saddleback Church in Lake Forest, California, has joined the cyber-church club. Their online church allows visitors to watch or join live streams from other campuses in Berlin, Buenos Aires, Hong Kong, and South Manila.

Andrew Conrad writes, "Today's online churches treat the internet as a campus all its own, with interactive chat, dedicated online pastors, and a web ministry ready to serve their cyber-congregation." Which means, like televangelists of an earlier era, there are a growing number of electronic congregations. For example, Joel and Victoria Osteen's Lakewood Churches have 43,000 members that attend only on-screen.[2]

This on-screen option is an important resource for people with mobility challenges and for many seniors. However, as cyber-congregations with visitations from online pastors continue to grow, it is difficult to predict to what extent it will replace face-to-face community gatherings. Even some local churches in the non-Western church are joining these online communities.

Join the Three-Step Dance

Now we will invite Christian leaders and those you work with to join the dance . . . **anticipate** some of the changes your churches, your people, and organizations could face if present trends continue as we race into the 2020s. For

---

2. Andrew Conrad, "5 Biggest Online Churches," Capterra, May 10, 2019, https://tinyurl.com/shv39rr.

one last time we will invite you and those you work with to **reflect** on some of the societal and biblical issues before you that you need to grapple with in order to respond faithfully to these challenges and opportunities. We will reflect briefly on our theology of missiology but spend most of our time **reflecting** on a theology of formation. The reason for this is that there is a direct link between the growing crisis of participation in our churches and the growing seduction that an aggressive consumer culture poses, a culture that would like to persuade us to invest more of our time and resources into another view of "hope."

Finally, we will survey some more examples of how Christian leaders and their teams are responding to these troubled times with **innovative** responses that welcome change to people's lives by creating new forms of church-making.

We want to end this book by encouraging you to continue doing the Three-Step Dance of **Anticipating**, **Reflecting**, and **Innovating**. We also urge you to take regular time to search for best practices as you plan. Join those Christian leaders who are embracing new disciplines for themselves and their colleagues and developing new habits. For example, could researchers in some seminaries and colleges near you help you start the search? Create a network of colleagues who will be able to put you in contact with those finding new ways forward.

Urging Leaders to Welcome the Good News Generation!

All Christian leaders know about what the Pew Research Center has categorized as the "nones and dones" of Gen Y and Z. We all know that these two incoming generations have the lowest rates of church affiliation. However, leaders in Silicon Valley firms are aware about other characteristics of Gen Y and Z that most church leaders aren't.

Because these two generations are the first digital generations, they are much more aware of and concerned about the issues of economic, racial, and environmental justice. Christian leaders need to realize these generations not only care, but a higher percentage want to *do* something about these issues. Some Silicon Valley firms have actually added a social mission to their corporate policies to attract this generation of compassionate and creative young leaders.

We will, at the end of this chapter, share some examples of how these young innovators are creating new social enterprises to empower neighbors at the margins. Dwight and Tom will also suggest that church planters should consider starting their projects by inviting the youth in their communities to become involved in neighborhood change-making way before trying to create a worshiping community. Let's start by identifying some of those changes and challenges that are likely to face our churches as we race into the 2020s.

Anticipating . . . The Rise of the Majority Church

In his book *Future Faith*, Wesley Granberg-Michaelson states:

> Today, Christianity is undergoing another historic shift. For the first time in more than one thousand years, a majority of the world's Christians are living in the Global South. This trend is accelerating, constituting the most dramatic geographical shift in the history of Christianity. For four hundred years, a

Western culture shaped by the Enlightenment has been the comfortable home for dominant expressions of Christianity in the world. Now that all of this is changing, Christianity has become predominately a non-western religion.[3]

As a Christian leader, what are the implications of this dramatic shift for your church and denomination as we move further into the twenty-first century?

Here is an example of the good news of leadership shifting to the global church. Micah Global is a great model of a new majority-world-led Christian organization. They are one of the faith-based organizations leading the way into being more faithfully present to the particular gifts brought to the world through each culture and people. Micah Global is an organization that was birthed as a hope-filled alternative to the political and economic colonizing impulses of Christendom's missions predominantly led by white westerners from the USA, Canada, and Western Europe. From Micah Global's inception, it drew on the leadership and influence of leaders from the majority church[4] to create this organization committed to integral mission.[5] Micah Global seeks to fan the flame of global richness at the heart of its innovation all over the planet.

Granberg-Michaelson's insights are simultaneously convincing and hopeful.[6] This global shift to the majority world

---

3. Wesley Granberg-Michaelson, *Future Faith: Ten Challenges Reshaping Christianity in the 21st Century* (Minneapolis: Fortress Press, 2017), 1–2.

4. "Majority" world/church refers to non-Western perspectives, cultures, and worldviews, which are the majority of the world's human population. It serves as a corrective for the hegemonic and colonizing force of the West on the rest of the globe.

5. Micah Global, www.micahnetwork.org.

6. It's important for us to note that Granberg-Michaelson was not the only one to highlight the shift to the global south. Philip Jenkins's book *The Next Christendom: The Coming of the Global Christianity* (Oxford: Oxford University Press, 2002) was a groundbreaker as well.

represents a very important ecclesial transformation that has tremendous potential. This shift may well be signaling the end of the Christendom era. Thanks be to God! Yet what does the church look like post-Christendom? Dwight encourages leaders in Western churches to learn what this means.

The seeds of the Christendom church can be traced back to the church's collusion with Rome beginning in the fourth century under Emperor Constantine. And when Rome fell to the "barbarians," the church emerged holding just enough power to keep parts of the Western cultural world functioning. The Christendom church was coming into its own. One of the unintended consequences of the church trying to love and serve through a season of remarkable cultural upheaval was a deepening entanglement of the church with political power.

It's taken a long time to decenter the Christendom church and its systems, but it's happening, and the whole world feels it.[7] You and your group feel it. To open up to

---

7. Arguably, the first major challenge to the hegemonic leadership of the Christendom church came in the seventh century through the birth of Islam, which introduced the first serious alternative narrative to the story being told by the Christendom church. The next challenge was an internal one, in 1054, when the leaders of the Eastern church (now known as the Orthodox tradition) tried and failed to confront the Western church's power grab. The cultural revolution of the Renaissance and its religious twin, the Protestant Reformation, were the next to challenge the Christendom church's power through personal reason, encapsulated in Martin Luther's famous words, "Here I stand!" Prior to the Renaissance it would have been unthinkable for an individual person to stand against the Christendom church's power. Looking back, we can clearly see that the Protestant Reformation was as much a political reformation as it was a theological reformation. Many of the Protestant "denominations" that emerged as distinctive from the Roman Catholic Church in the wake of the reformation were about alternate polities, or distribution of power. In fact, the alternative power polities reflected the societal birth of the rule of law, nation/state, and representational and democratic forms of governance, often visible in the names of the new denominations: Presbyterian, Brethren, Congregational, Free Church, etc. By the time we get to the seventeenth-century Enlightenment, human reason was not taking any of

perspectives and experiences of Christ beyond Eurocentric Christianity is actually a divine gift. To attend carefully, with humility and with gratitude to the wisdom, concerns, and leadership of followers of the Way of Jesus in the new majority church is an audacious invitation to love God as we learn to love our global neighbors.

Anticipating . . . the Incredible Shrinking Western Church

It doesn't seem that long ago that the Western church was optimistic that a new wave of church planting might reverse the evident rate of decline in the church. In the late 1980s and into the early 2000s, we began to see the "emerging church-planting movement," originating in Britain. It also drew energy and momentum from the missional movement.[8] They were relational and experimental, involved in the arts, and were into more narrative than propositional theology. In the mid-1990s, this emerging church movement spread to Australia, New Zealand, and came alive in North America through the lives and work of Brian McLaren, Karen Ward, and Doug Pagitt, together with a host of other young North Americans.

However, as the emerging church movement slowly ended in the mid-2000s, we were awakened by a new real-

---

the claims of the Christendom church at face value. The Enlightenment not only opened up space for humanism, therapy, and public atheism, but it set the stage for the obsolescence of the Christendom religion as a whole by polarizing Social Gospel liberals and Bible-believing fundamentalists. Thanks be to God that the Spirit of God has never given up chipping away at the hegemony of Eurocentric church systems. Christ's church is just that—Christ's church. No one culture or race gets to determine orthodoxy, orthopraxy, or polity.

8.   Tom Sine, *The New Conspirators: Creating the Future One Mustard Seed at a Time* (Downers Grove, IL: InterVarsity Press, 2008), 35.

ity; not only were mainline churches graying and weakening, more evangelical churches were, too. Sometimes it can be helpful to have a benchmark, so we thought it might be helpful to look at a few statistics from where the church was during the rise of the emerging church movement.

In Britain, the Christian Research Association stated that church attendance was 8.1 percent of the country's population in 1995 and was projected to decline to 7.7 percent in 2000. The same research organization reported that church attendance has now declined to 5.5 percent in 2019 and is still declining.[9] In Australia, attendance was at 10 percent in 1999. Today, it has declined to 7 percent and is still declining, according to National Church Life Survey Research.[10]

Kirk Hadaway, chief statistician for the United Church of Christ, reported in the late 1990s that church attendance in the United States had declined to 24 percent, down from a 40 percent figure that would have been accurate back in the 1970s. *Outreach* magazine, drawing on research from the Covenant Church, placed attendance in 2018 at 17.7 percent and still declining. *Outreach* also reported that less than 20 percent of Americans attend churches regularly.[11] If our churches in the West don't find a vital approach to both renewing vital faith and re-creating churches that are more focused on serious change-making, then by the 2030s we could wind up with a lot of empty structures.

"Over the past decade," *The Atlantic* announced in 2017, "pollsters charted something remarkable: Americans— long known for their piety—were fleeing religion in

9. Sine, *The New Conspirators*, 128.

10. NCLS, www.ncls.org.au › topic › church-attendance.

11. "7 Startling Facts: An Up Close Look at Church Attendance in America," *Outreach Magazine*, April 10, 2018, https://tinyurl.com/y35vlxr2.

increasing numbers. The vast majority still believe in God. But the share that rejected organized religious affiliation is growing fast, rising from 6% in 1992 to 22% in 2014. Among millennials the figure is 35%."[12]

In spite of *The Atlantic*'s commentary regarding declining religious affiliation, the good news is that a broad range of denominations and church-planting groups in Western countries are changing their approach to pioneering new Christian faithful communities. That said, there is little indication, at this time, that this important effort is going to significantly slow the decline. The legacy of the Western churches' colonization appears to be catching up with it.

That many of Christendom churches are graying and declining doesn't tell the whole story of decline. Churches are also experiencing declining levels of giving and volunteering. A number of congregations are spending a greater proportion of their resources on property maintenance than on ministry to the congregation or their wider community.

Anticipating . . . the Economic Impact of Rapid Decline

John Dorhauer, General Minister and President of the United Church of Christ, wrote a very challenging and candid book on the future of the UCC that is dealing with very rapid decline in membership and resources, *Beyond Resistance: The Institutional Church Meets the Postmodern World.*[13]

The painful decisions some UCC churches were facing

---

12. Peter Beinart, "Breaking Faith: The Culture War over Religious Morality Has Faded; In Its Place Ss Something Much Worse," *The Atlantic*, April 2017.

13. John Dorhauer, *Beyond Resistance: The Institutional Church Meets the Postmodern World* (Chicago: Exploration Press, 2015).

stood out most in this book. Congregations in other Christian denominations are facing similar painful decisions. The declining numbers in the UCC are further exacerbated by the double whammy of high costs and shrinking income. Dorhauer reported that congregations are being forced to choose to reduce their pastor's salary in order to retain adequate resources to keep the building cleaned and maintained. Other denominations are also facing some similar challenges that are likely to grow worse as congregations continue to gray and decline.

Another example relates to the retirement program of those employed working in Catholic Charities. Many paid into retirement programs only to later discover that the funds were not set aside for retirement. Instead, these funds were reportedly used to cover the costs of the institutions where they were employed.

According to Scott James, "At issue is a law passed by Congress in 1974 that exempted religious organizations from federal laws that regulated and guaranteed pensions. Decades later, the effects of the lack of oversight are surfacing."[14] In talking to leaders of seminaries across the country, many are facing an economic crisis too. Since seminary grads can no longer be assured of a full-time position at a church, student enrollment is dropping. As a consequence of declining clergy candidate enrollment, seminaries are scrambling to prepare a new generation for other vocations such as community activists and social workers. Some seminary leaders are reporting they may not be able to find an economically viable way to sustain their programs in the 2020s.

Adding to this crisis is the fact that many young clergy

---

14. Scott James, "Faith in a 'Hidden Paycheck' That Could Vanish for Good," *New York Times*, September 12, 2019, F7.

who are graduating with seminary debt of $80–100,000 are having to work bi-vocationally, since a growing number of established congregations and new church starts can't afford to pay a pastor a full-time salary.

These challenges make it more and more important that denominational leaders help their declining congregations anticipate five to seven years ahead, so that they can proactively steward the legacy of local church-owned properties. Congregations need to look carefully at their demographic and giving trends in order to help make hard choices about their futures, including responsible ways they can be missional and serve their context while furthering the mission of their tradition. When aging churches wait too long to anticipate the future, there is often little energy for innovation left.

Anticipating . . . Retracting Rates of Participation and Giving

When pastor Randy Bursma of First Christian Reformed Church in Grand Rapids was asked about attendance patterns at the church, he replied, "We have always been a 'two-fer' church." If you're wondering, like we were, what a "two-fer" church is, Randy defines it this way: "A two-fer church used to mean attending Sunday morning and Sunday night. Now it means twice a month." People are giving less time and money to their churches today. People vote with their time and finances. As we have seen, other values are increasingly shaping our sense of what is important and what is of value.

We have heard leaders in a range of both mainline Protestant and evangelical churches report that their member attendance patterns are declining. They also report that their members have less time for formative practices such as prayer, scripture reflection, and service within the church or in their neighborhood.

According to the University of Maryland, volunteering in the larger society in the United States is at a fourteen-year low.[15] People are working more hours and earning less. Many are spending significant time in long commutes. In many churches more part-time people are hired to lead the community in things that volunteers would have led in generations past.

The State of Church Giving Report has published twenty-eight reports that map out church finances. Their reporting started in 1968 by sampling a broad selection of denominations in the United States. It reports both individual giving to the church and the percentage of benevolence giving to local and global sources. In 1968 the percentage of American church contributions that went to benevolence was 64 percent; in 2016 it was down to 36 percent. This is a shocking decline, since the overall wealth for the middle class in the US appreciated significantly from 1968 to 2016.[16]

However, a report in the *Stanford Innovation Review* states that many faith-based nonprofits such as the Salvation Army and Catholic Charities are seeing their giving increase.[17] Could this be signaling a shift in trust from local Christendom churches to more nonprofit organizations that address the benevolent needs of a place and its people?

---

15. Kaitlin Ahmad, "Fewer Americans Are Volunteering and Giving Than Any Time in the Last Two Decades," Phys.Org, November 15, 2018, https://tiny url.com/uklrxzq.

16. John and Sylvia Ronsvalle, *The State of Church Giving through 2016: What Do Denominational Leaders Want to Do with 8 Billion More a Year?* (Champaign, IL: Empty Tomb Association, 2018), 3.

17. Faculty of the Lily School of Philanthropy, "8 Myths of US Philanthropy," *Stanford Social Innovation Review* (Fall 2019): 29.

How could this become a design opportunity for church leaders today to create more new churches that are focused not on charity but on creating new **innovative** forms of neighborhood empowerment?

What else might this era of accelerating decline in giving and attendance invite from local churches, denominations, Christian colleges, and seminaries? What kinds of other leadership skills might this invite?

Reflecting . . . On What It Means to Be the Church in the 2020s

Many leaders in our churches, mission organizations, and denominations can remember the growing call that began with the publishing of the classic *The Missional Church* written by Darrel Guder and five other missiologists in 1998. It called on all our churches to view North America as a mission field and to become more outwardly focused on mission. It had a remarkable impact. In response, many denominations started investing in widespread church planting.[18]

Numbers of churches also started investing more in reaching out to those in need in their neighborhoods. One Covenant congregation in an interracial community actually radically altered their budget to free up 50 percent of their income to invest in the urban empowerment work of an economic nonprofit they started. Members were gratified by the difference it made in the lives of their neighbors. A number of other churches also increased their investment in global mission.

---

18. Darrel Guder, *Missional Church: A Vision for the Sending of the Church in North America* (Grand Rapids: Eerdmans, 1998).

Two decades later, Guder looked back on the broad range of missional activities in local churches, church planting, and ongoing missional conversations and concluded, "By all accounts the project's intention has been realized."

However, in looking back, Guder also reflected on British theologian Lesslie Newbigin's perspective about how the context for Christianity in Western culture had been secularized: "His question motivated the Gospel and Culture Network to seek research support for an intensive engagement of this challenge."[19]

Guder, **reflecting** on this challenge, states the following in *Gospel Reductionism and Modernity*:

> As the Enlightenment stressed the autonomy of human reason . . . it contributed in its own way to the reduction of the Gospel. The road to salvation was the schooling of the human mind and the formation of a moral person. The goal was, as hallowed in our public traditions, "the pursuit of happiness." The Enlightenment defined the norms and expectations of this brave new world of humanism . . . Nor did man have any higher purpose than the attainment of his own happiness.[20]

Time to Reflect Again on "What Is the Good Life?"

As we witness the accelerating decline in church attendance, volunteering, giving, and participation in spiritual practices, Guder's comments move us to examine once again whether it is possible that our notion of the good life

---

19.   Darrell Guder, "The Missional Conversation Twenty Years Later," Catalyst, March 15, 2018, https://tinyurl.com/sf5qlgv.

20.   Darrell Guder, *Gospel Reductionism and Modernity*, Salt Light and a City (Eugene, OR: Cascade, 2017).

is shaped more by the aspirations and values of modernity than by the gospel of Jesus. Is it possible this is playing a major role in our declining participation in our faith and practices?

Recall James K. A. Smith's encouragement to be aware of what we love in chapter 4. We also need to reflect on where our notions of the good life come from. Smith states, "We need to become aware of our immersions. This is the water' you've been swimming in your whole life. We need to recognize that our imaginations and longings are not impervious to our environments and only informed by our (supposedly 'critical') thinking." Smith insists, "To the contrary, our loves and imaginations are conscripted by all sorts of liturgies that are loaded with a vision of the good life."[21]

Reflecting on How the Values of Modernity Could Accelerate the Rate of Decline

In *Out of Babylon*, Walter Brueggemann offers us some important insights about how our context can influence our values more often than we realize. He reflects on the current reality that Christians in America are facing. He likens it to the captivity the Jews experienced at the hands of another empire, the Persians. "Given this 'Persian' model we are invited to think of the church in the United States as a practitioner of 'accommodation' . . . because we already specialize in selling out to the dominant culture." He adds, "The church has mostly positioned itself so that the promises of the Gospel are readily lined out as the 'Amer-

---

21.   Smith, *You Are What You Love*, 38.

ican Dream' with endless choices and bottomless entitle-ments."[22]

A number of leaders in the church in the United States are deeply concerned about the graying and declining of the American church and are attempting to challenge both leaders and members to identify what may be distracting them from their devotion to God and their service to neighbors.

J. R. Briggs, a Christian author and church-planting consultant with Fresh Expressions, was asked, "What do you see as the biggest challenges to effective discipleship in the American church?" Briggs responded,

As I coach and mentor pastors all over the country, I frequently see and hear five major challenges to discipleship in the American church:

(1) the seductive pull of consumerism;

(2) the enormous amount of distraction, particularly with technology;

(3) a lack of clear and robust theology of suffering;

(4) the belief in the lie that the American Dream is the most fulfilling and satisfying expression of true life; and

(5) an unwillingness by pastors to make the sacrifices necessary to see people discipled into the Way of Jesus—even if it means losing or leaving their ministry positions.[23]

---

22. Walter Brueggemann, *Out of Babylon* (Nashville: Abingdon Press, 2010), 141.

23. James P. Long, "Bobby Harrington: Culture and Discipleship," *Outreach Magazine*, March 20, 2017, https://tinyurl.com/ude2uyk.

William T. Cavanaugh in *Economics and Christian Desire* states that the biblical worldview sees human desires as fundamentally social and not consumerist.[24] The increasingly commercial character of our culture tends to make us and our youth much more vulnerable to the advertising that is designed to shape our aspirations and values to a very different notion of the good life. But the good life proclaimed by Jesus and his disciples was one of a radical hospitality that reached out to others across race, class, and nationality to welcome others into their homes and into their Christian communities. For Christians in the West, we seem to be largely blind to the fact that our social values are shaped more by the values of popular culture than by the way of Jesus and the earliest community of the disciples.

For three decades Tom taught a course on "Christian Worldview" at Fuller Seminary's Seattle campus, and he would say that hands down the toughest issue Christians face was struggling with the informed notion of the nature of the "good life." It is so much easier to let popular culture define the good life for us and keep our faith in a separate box, isn't it? Thoughtful students with highly developed theologies had rarely reflected on the tensions between their theological views and the insistent values of popular culture. When the class focused on theological topics such as atonement or the Eucharist, they had some differences but little real discord. However, when the class attempted to examine theological values and the values of our modern consumer culture, things got tense. They all struggled, including the professor. We encourage both leaders and those preparing to be leaders to take time to reflect on the

---

24.   William T. Cavanaugh, *Being Consumed: Economics and Christian Desire* (Grand Rapids: Eerdmans, 2008).

growing tensions between biblical values and the increasingly invasive values of this new tech culture on us and our young.

Reflecting: On the Call to Be the Church in the 2020s

As the decline of the Western church continues, many Christians are asking important questions like: Why go to church? What is the mission of the church? What is the church? Or more generally, what's the point of church anyway?

We wonder, as we work with Christian leaders, if the decline of the church in the West isn't really an opportunity to call followers of Jesus to a more engaged, whole-life faith. Dwight reminds us, from the important work of the New Parish, that the church is a cluster of Christ followers who gather to learn the way of love and faithful presence within an ecosystem of relationships that is the neighborhood. They gather to discern together who the Holy Spirit is inviting them to become and who they might partner with to make more visible the shalom of God. Together, faith communities learn, practice, and dare each other to live lives of holistic faithful presence with God, with each other, with neighbors, with the creation and the local built environment, with economic systems, and with systems of power or oppression. The church is that local community seeking to keep in step with the Holy Spirit right where it is in the everyday, ordinary stuff of life. They look fearlessly at the reality of where they are and what is happening, prayerfully discerning a way forward together. It may well be that the decline of the Christendom church we are witnessing in the

Western world is a sign that God is refounding the church for the refounding of society.[25]

We love the church in all its forms, and we have spent most of our lives serving Christ by trying to understand and trying to serve Christ's church. We are heartened that in many of these faith communities the center of "community life," "formational life," and "missional life" is not the gathered church, but rather the followers of Christ in their everyday lives. These faith communities help each Christ follower enter the ordinary stuff with a different imagination, a different value set, a different measure of success . . . a more shalomic imagination!

We have taken a little time to anticipate some of the new challenges and opportunities that are likely to face us in our lives, congregations, and communities as we race into the 2020s, a decade of accelerating change. We have also reflected on some of the things that are undermining our levels of investment in our lives and congregations in our devotion to God and our care for our neighbors. It is now time to join those leaders that are creating **innovative** expressions of church for the turbulent 2020s. We want to take you on a quick tour of some young innovators and a range of **innovative** churches that are involved in being a difference and making a difference.

Innovating as Christ's Church

Let's take a quick tour of some of the most **innovative** expressions of church engaging some of the new waves of change. We begin by introducing you to a new generation

---

25.   Alan J. Roxburgh and Martin Robinson, *Practices for the Refounding of God's People: The Missional Challenge of the West* (New York: Church Publishing, 2018).

of compassionate, **innovative** leaders who will be taking over leadership of our churches, Christian ministries, and neighborhood change-making. We will also take you on a quick tour of some established churches that found some surprising new ways to innovate.

If you are pastors, lay leaders, nonprofit, or denominational leaders looking for new possibilities, we hope some of these examples will ignite your imaginations and motivate you to address incoming waves of change.

Innovating as Church . . . Reimagining Property Stewardship

It seems clear that the future of the church will focus less on the construction and maintenance of buildings, so centrally important in the past. At the same time, existing church properties can also be incredible resources if stewarded in **innovative** ways for the future. We will share a couple examples of alternative uses of church properties and alternatives to buildings for the churches for tomorrow.

Dwight has been researching an array of remarkable new models for repurposing church properties at The Seattle School of Theology and Psychology, where he teaches. The project is titled "Here for Good: Flipping the Script on Churched-Owned Properties." His framing question is, "How can local churches reimagine property stewardship so that the asset of their church-owned building can fund their ministry instead of the people needing to fund their building?"[26]

As Christian churches continue to age and shrink in

---

26.   Unpublished research proposal by Dwight J. Friesen, 2019.

attendance, the economics of ministry are rendering growing numbers of churches financially at-risk. Some fall into disrepair, some are sold, and some are even abandoned. Some local churches are flipping the script of their church-owned property. These churches are discovering **innovative** ways to leverage the asset of their property to fund their church and ministry. Dwight's research project constructively reframes this looming crisis as a profound neighborhood opportunity rooted in deep listening to the place in which the church property is located.

Innovating: Sampling New Models Making a Difference in the 2020s

Here, then, are a few examples of how churches have made a real difference in the lives of their neighbors, starting with one striking example of how to repurpose church property in downtown Los Angeles.

Worship in a Parking Lot

First United Methodist Church in Los Angeles was struggling with a problem afflicting churches all over North America. They possessed a large building that was expensive to maintain, and the congregation was aging and declining in attendance. For many shrinking congregations, buildings maintenance takes up a growing share of their limited income.

Pastor Mandy McDow, the minister of First United Methodist Church, introduced the congregation to what she calls "the inverted business model." Essentially, their historic building was deconstructed to create a 100-space car park across the street from LA's 20,000-seat arena.

In this "inverted business model," the church community earns a very good income through collecting parking fees for sporting events and concerts at night. The income from the parking lot not only pays the modest costs for the church, but the church is also able to provide generous amounts of this income to social service agencies in downtown LA to address the needs of their neighbors. On Sundays, the parking lot is transformed. They raise a tent to hold their worship service.

Enterprise Community Partners . . . Church Properties to Low-Income Housing

In the Mid-Atlantic region of the United States, this new "inverted economic model" is helping address the urgent and growing need of low-income housing. Enterprise Community Partners is one of the firms that is repurposing church properties. Sometimes, they create a community space in the housing complex that the church can use as a worship space on Sundays. Pastor McDow is deeply concerned by the number of pastors negatively affected by their congregations' struggles with the costs of property maintenance: "For McDow it is down to the question she regularly asks herself: 'How do we best love God and one another?'"[27]

---

27.   Hillary Frances, "A Church That Doesn't Need Your Money," *Sojourners*, December 2018, 35, 37.

Candace McDuffie writes, "When singer and entrepreneur Pharrell Williams' inaugural music festival debuted in New York in April, it boasted a high-profile list of performers including Missy Elliot, Gwen Stefani, and Busta Rhymes. But it also featured something else: spirituality. Black millennials, in particular, are seeking such opportunities. This is prompting more 'church time' at black music events. For example, Kanye West led a service at this year's Coachella."[28] Even though these music festivals aren't churches *per se*, they seem to be providing an opportunity for music and spiritual engagement for young people who are looking for a more vital faith.

Pew Research discovered African American millennials are more religious than other millennials. Four in ten say they attend services weekly. However, "many millennials have walked away from organized religion because it has been rooted in a lot of pain and trauma," says Ms. Benhow, who hosts her own podcast, *Red Lip Theology*.

In response to this growing interest among young African American followers of the Jesus Way in connecting spirituality through art, Smithsonian's National Museum of African American History and Culture has started a conversation series called *GOD-Talk*. These events are designed to empower African American young people to reclaim and, in some cases, rediscover their story. "The conversation series looks at how black millennials are defining and redefining spirituality to create communities that are more

---

28.   Candace McDuffie, "For Church-Shy Black Millennials, Music Festivals Offer Faith," *Christian Science Monitor*, May 20, 2019, 37. Pharrell's first water festival was held April 26–28, 2019, in Virginia Beach.

equitable, inclusive, and compassionate," said Brad Braxton, Director of the Center.[29]

Broad Street–Urban Hospitality Center

Though we have both worked with a lot of urban churches, neither of us has ever seen anything quite like Broad Street Ministry in Philadelphia, formerly Center City Presbyterian Church. While there, we met Laura Colee, who is both the administrator and pastor. The church decided to redesign their church building to offer a broad range of services for their downtown neighbors. Here is what they offer:

- Meals for 300 people, five days a week. Several local professional chefs regularly come in to share their gifts. A Jamaican chef who prepares large vats of Jamaican jerked chicken is a big favorite. Laura reports that meatless Monday is the least popular meal of the week.

- Concierge caseworkers

- Primary care doctors

- A clothing closet that they keep well stocked

- A mailbox where people can receive their mail

- An overnight café that has hot coffee and rolls, which can handle 75 to 100 guests per night, though on cold nights they have accommodated as many as 300 people

---

29. "God-Talk: A Black Millennials and Faith Conversation," National Museum of African American History and Culture, accessed April 11, 2020, https://tinyurl.com/vbynzz8.

- Open worship every Sunday at 4:00 p.m. with communion

Isn't it encouraging to see established churches reinvent themselves and their properties to creatively engage the changing needs of their neighborhoods?

A Church-Loving Bristol

Let's head across the pond to visit Love Bristol in the UK, a group that loves their community in a range of very surprising but welcome ways. Love Bristol's motto is "Shop Local, Pray Local." Like Broad Street in Philly, Love Bristol is all about inventing ways to serve their very immediate community.

Downtown Bristol is a very different community from downtown Philly. In the 1990s, Bristol was a hub of art and music, with street artists such as Banksy and Robert Del Naja (also known as 3D). Two decades later, the neighborhood became home to artisan coffee shops and craft ale, plus a number of local shops that include a community grocery. No stained glass or signs visibly indicate that this grocery store is also a church.

Love Bristol has, in recent years, sought to serve its neighbors in a range of quite imaginative ways. For example, they have created Love Bristol social enterprises such as Love Windows, where unemployed young people are trained to become professional window washers.

Love Bristol Studios hosts desk space for graphic designers, trainers, coders, computer whizzes, and app developers, plus multi-use spaces for local artists and designers to display their creations. The Elemental Collective features in their grocery store local produce, fresh milk and eggs, locally grown flowers, and locally produced yogurt and juices. Not surprisingly, they also sell locally roasted coffee.

Some Crofts is a boutique charity shop with donated shoes and clothing. They host educational projects for young people and they even host a literature festival.

Above all, Love Bristol is an established church that has a high level of investment in their local community. It appears to be a contemporary expression of the UK charismatic house church movement from the '80s and '90s. Here is their purpose statement:

- *We are people-centred.* Love, grace, and mercy expressed to each other and others around us through friendships and support. We want to do life together, acting as family for one another, nurturing and challenging each other in a journey of faith. Hospitality, inclusion, accountability, random acts of kindness is the flavour. Relationships with people in our local neighborhood, mutual respect and an openness about our pursuit of a life with Jesus. Committed to loving people on the margins who are often overlooked, we want to invest in these friendships and offer practical support wherever we can.

- *We are prayer-driven.* We aspire to be a community with prayer as the foundation of all that we do and as an offering to those around us.

- *We are Spirit-filled.* A community that is filled and overflowing with the Holy Spirit is alive. We need that to do what we do. We believe God is always speaking and we enjoy the twists and turns of our adventures being led by his voice, calling us into more freedom and a sacrificial lifestyle.

- *We are rooted in compassion.* We aim to be a community that chooses mercy over judgment, regarding each other and those around us.[30]

Love Bristol has also purchased properties where some members live in intentional community. When they worship, their band reportedly turns up the sound and things get shaking. Love Bristol is under the "umbrella" of a larger church called Woodland that has a community of 1,800 members.[31]

Fresh Expressions is an **innovative** church-planting movement that started in the UK but is now very active in creative church-planting in the United States. Heather Evans, who works with Grace Church Cape Coral in Florida, discovered that numbers of seniors who retired in Florida are struggling with isolation and loneliness, so Heather and her Fresh Expressions team planted a dinner church at the second largest mobile home park in the nation. You can learn more about the **innovative** work and national conferences of Fresh Expressions at www.freshexpressionsus.org.

Chris Morton, who works in strategic planning for Fresh Expressions, said, "By 2024, we hope to see the majority of established denominations committed to equipping and empowering pioneers who will experiment with fresh expressions. We also hope to continue to develop tangible models such as Dinner Church (http://dinnerchurch.com) that are easy for churches to grasp and experiment with."[32]

---

30.   LoveBristol, https://www.lovebristol.org.

31.   Joel Duddell, "Would Jesus Be a Gentrifier? How Christianity Is Embracing Urban Renewal," *The Guardian*, March 7, 2017.

32.   Chris Morton, email message to author, February 14, 2020.

V3 Network Getting Innovative in the Marketplace

Marketplace planting is a new form of church planting being initiated by the V3 Movement,[33] which seeks to break down the sacred/secular divide by drawing on the Trappist monk model of starting businesses that contribute to the common good, gaining respect in the business community, discerning what God is doing, and seeking to join it as well as discipline those who express and interest.

Innovating as Church . . . Leaning into the Coming Challenges

Tod Bolsinger, a vice president at Fuller Theological Seminary, has written an important book for Christian leaders we mentioned earlier, *Canoeing the Mountains: Christian Leadership in Uncharted Territory*. He uses the metaphor of Lewis and Clark's exploration of the American West to reflect on how to overcome seemingly impossible challenges to reach a destination. Essentially, Bolsinger is challenging leaders to become much more adaptive in navigating our rapidly changing world.[34] The post-Christendom cultural context invites a far more **innovative** church. Many of the Christendom church's structures and systems don't appear to be up to the adaptive challenge of this era of accelerating change, but you and your group likely are. You are willing to follow Christ into the uncharted waters of the future.

This is important encouragement for today's church

---

33.   Tom Sine is a contributor to the V3 blog.

34.   Bolsinger, *Canoeing the Mountains.*

leaders. Christopher James, in *Church Planting in Post-Christian Soil*, gives us a brief description of how the context for church planting[35] is changing and how it could indicate similar changes in other urban communities. James describes some of the challenges that church planters are likely to face not only in Seattle, but also in other post-Christian urban communities.[36] "Historian Jan Shipps describes characteristics of Seattle that could be a harbinger of urban communities in the future," James writes, adding, "the Seattle context reflects characteristics that could become true for other regions including increasing urbanization, progressivism, the digital revolution and post-Christian religious dynamics."[37]

Innovating as Church . . . Good News Generation Innovators Leading the Way

We are going to quickly introduce you to some innovators from Gen Y and Z expressing their strong desire to enable their vulnerable neighbors to become economically self-

---

35.   There is a great deal of renewed interest in pioneering new church expressions (though we're beginning to notice the decline of "church planting" language) that more meaningfully emerge from the particularity of local context, so as to more authentically serve the local. There is a broad range of church-planting organizations. For example, Fresh Expressions has been involved in the UK for decades and is a major planter in North America too. The US church-planting organizations include the V3 Network, Missio Alliance, and major denominations such as ELCA, Presbyterians, United Methodists, Southern Baptists, and Four Square.

36.   There is a subtle but important distinction between post-Christian and post-Christendom. Post-Christian seeks to describe the loss of the primacy of a Christian worldview especially in the West in favor of worldviews like secularism or nationalism. Although Christendom can broadly refer to a Christian-majority country, it usually connotes a collision of power between church and state.

37.   Christopher B. James, *Church Planting in Post Christian Soil: Theology and Practice* (Oxford: Oxford University Press, 2019), 13–14.

reliant. You will understand why we call them "the good news generation." They are creating possibilities for both change-making and church-making. We invite others in Gen Next to join them!

Gen Y and Z Making a Difference in Grand Rapids: Treetops Collective

Dana Doll studied International Development at Calvin College before working in northern Uganda. On her return to the United States she discovered other women who were interested in the same kind of development work she had experienced in Uganda. Doll said, "We started by asking questions. How can the world do a better job of welcoming refugees? How can we answer that question in our own community? How can we be a city where refugee women can sink their roots down and flourish with their families for generations to come?"

Doll and Treetops Collective passionately believe that each of their new neighbors has gifts, skills, and dreams that make their city better. Their organization's mission is to connect these women to people and opportunities so they can flourish for generations to come.[38] Just as trees need the right soil and conditions, so do strong women. As they become established and stable, they provide shade for others, prevent erosion, and provide numerous other benefits to their surroundings.

Doll said, "I love working with refugee women because I know what it is like to feel unwelcome in a new place." She explained that Treetops Collective and all the young volunteers that work there are attempting to enable these new

---

38.   www.TreeTopsCollective.org.

American women to become more sustainable by training them in skills needed to earn a livable income. Doll said, "We believe as they flourish, our city will flourish."[39]

Justin Beene: Grand Rapids Center for Community Transformation

The other **innovative** individual is Justin Beene. Like Doll, Beene is also a millennial. Beene founded and is the director for the Grand Rapids Center for Community Transformation. Recently, Beene focused the Center's efforts on empowering young people. African American young people ages sixteen to twenty-four in Grand Rapids were experiencing an alarming 25 percent unemployment rate. Through an **innovative** collaboration of business, church, social enterprises, nonprofit organizations, and scores of residents, Beene and his team seek to "create opportunities for transformation through meaningful relationships, work, education, and community development."[40] Two of their initiatives include Rising Grinds, which not only serves quality coffee but fosters entrepreneurial capacity in young people, and Youth Build, a process to train young people in the construction trades.[41]

While neither of these two leaders are church planters in the Christendom sense, they are profound examples of innovating as Christ's church—people living in the shalomic way of Jesus who see trending data, reflect on God's dream for creation, and courageously innovate.

---

39.   www.TreeTopsCollective.org.

40.   www.grcct.com/.

41.   www.grcct.com/.

Social Enterprise to Church Planting

We encourage new church innovators to consider the advice of Sean Benesh in his recent book, *Navigating the Intersection of Church Planting and Social Entrepreneurship*. He has invested in a very unusual form of church planting. After years of working in urban empowerment, Benesh suggests that church innovators begin not by launching a worship gathering or starting a Bible study, but by launching a new social enterprise to enable those on the margins to become more economically self-reliant.

Benesh is on to something. When people in a neighborhood can see and feel the impact of shalomic imagination applied to the real challenges facing real people in a real place, good news is revealed. Hearts that were closed to religion or would never darken the door of a Christendom church's building open up and find fresh resonance with the **innovative** work of Christ's church. Sounds a bit like Jesus's words from the Sermon on the Mount: "Let your light shine before others, so that they may see your good works and give glory to your Father who is in heaven."[42]

Dwight and Ron Carucci made an unexpected discovery that supports Benesh's recommendation. After studying a number of successful start-up churches and Christian non-profits from around North America, they found that after at least ten years of ministry, the churches that had begun as a worship gathering never successfully developed a sustained missional identity. However, nearly all the churches and the nonprofits that began in missional/entrepreneurial service—even if not a church *per se*—eventually developed a formational and worship practice in order to sustain their

---

42.   Matthew 5:16 (ESV).

mission, community, and shalomic reason for existing.[43]
Shalomic action in the world breeds worship, yet Christendom worship systems may not breed mission.

Catacombs Change-Making Church

One of the church plants that have engaged the compassionate young are the Catacomb Communities. Essentially, these are smaller house churches started by the Northwest Washington Synod of ELCA.[44] Each congregation was designed to have eight to eleven members in a house-church setting. Catacomb communities typically meet twice a month for a meal, a liturgy, and a check-in for accountability, much as the early Methodist churches hosted. These groups are designed to enable members to share their daily struggles and ask others to hold them accountable in their journey with Jesus.

The Catacomb model enables its members to keep their costs down by meeting in homes where some of the members live, so there are no building maintenance costs. They also reduce costs by having lay members trained in ELCA churches to lead the liturgy, plan the gathering, and prepare the meal. There are no trained clergy.

But the real distinction in the Catacomb model is that the primary time these eight to eleven members spend together is not spent in their twice-a-month gatherings. Their primary time is spent in weekly change-making ven-

---

43. The Contextual Research project, conducted by Ron Carucci and Dwight J. Friesen, sought to test the hypothesis that organizational sustainability resulted from deep ongoing contextual listening and ongoing leadership/ organizational transformation. For the purposes of this study, "success" was defined by two primary factors: surviving as an organization for more than ten years, and having transitioned from first-generation to second-generation leadership.

44. https://tinyurl.com/wvokkfw.

tures called "community organizing." A Catacomb group in the agricultural community in Mount Vernon, Washington, discerned a very important community need among Latino farm workers. They discovered that they were not always well-paid and sometimes not at all.

So this Catacomb community helped the workers develop a website in Spanish and English and organize local meetings to share their stories and struggles with neighbors in Mount Vernon. It is evident why this kind of church might be of greater interest to the "good news generation" that is more interested in making a real difference in the lives of their neighbors than spending time and money on the property maintenance that many churches struggle with.

Valley Mountain Church: A Co-Working Space for Change-Making

John Helmiere is the pastor of a new Methodist church plant in Seattle. One of the things that makes this new plant unique is that they don't have a church building. John and his team decided instead to buy a building in an interracial neighborhood as a co-working space where a new and primarily young congregation worships on Sunday.

During the week, the Co-lab is a social co-working space that is rented out to help pay the bills. This is also an incubator for local change-making ventures. It is home to twenty local change-making organizations, an art gallery, a learning kitchen, and a homeless drop-in center. The members of Valley and Mountain describe this venture as "an organism for progressing onward as a hospitable, relevant, self-sustaining, and generative movement that reflects God's radically inclusive love."[45]

Doing the Three-Step Dance

We have valued journeying with you as we race into this decade of daunting new challenges for the larger world as well as the Western church and those of you who lead it. We hope you and those you work with are motivated to continue to dance with those who are creating **innovative** new ways to both be a difference and make a difference in the turbulent 2020s and beyond that authentically reflect the way of Jesus.

We Want to Hear from You!

We would value learning about how you are creating **innovative** strides toward your best lives, to make a difference in your community, to empower a new generation of innovators, or to motivate your church to create new ways to do neighborhood change-making.

We would welcome learning how you and those you work with, not only in local churches, but also colleges, seminaries, and campus ministry groups, are creating **innovative** ways to both be a difference and make a difference that challenges and reflects the compassion of Christ.

You can write us at www.newchangemakers.com. We will post a selection of innovations and comments that you send us. We will also post some examples at the New Parish Collective website, www.parishcollective.org.

We have enjoyed sharing some new opportunities and

---

45.   https://valleyandmountain.org.

creative new responses that reflect something of the shalom of God. We conclude our journey together with an invitation. You are invited with others in imagining new ways to give a fresh expression of hope in Jesus Christ that calls us beyond ourselves in these troubled times.

Prayer

Communal God,

As perfect community, you created us in and for community. You lovingly crafted human beings to need others. And through your incarnation in Jesus the Christ, you provided a glimpse into the kind of genuine fellowship we can actually come to know. And yet, loving communities sometimes feel rather elusive. We can't become people of love by ourselves. We need your Spirit, and we need others; basically, we need Christ's church. Help us discover afresh those around us who are seeking to live faithfully present in all relationships. In an era when our Christendom church structures are declining, help us to see such decline as a Holy Spirit design opportunity. We need fresh expressions of your church. Help us to innovate as Christ's church. Amen.

For Group Discussion

1. In what ways is new technology altering how the church operates as we race into this new high-tech future?

2. Is it possible that the Christendom era is ending and the church is becoming "a new majority-world" church?

3. How long can the Western church continue to decline in numbers, participation, devotion, and giving in the 2020s, until our local and global ministry is severely reduced?

4. What are some important biblical themes we need to reflect on to become more devoted to our God and more available to express the compassion of Christ in our congregations, our communities, and our world?

5. What are **innovative** ways to enable established churches to shift from charity to serious new forms of change-making both locally and globally?

6. As you read the examples of the new forms of both change-making and church-making created by the young, what are some ways you might invite the concerns and creativity of the young in your neighborhoods and congregations?

7. Could you host a gathering of both young innovators and concerned leaders to imagine and launch new expressions of church that are less involved in property management and more invested in being a difference and making a difference?

8. Could your church throw a new Advent party called "Surprised by Hope," where you create a celebration that gives creative expression to the images of hope in Isaiah 2:1–4 and 25:6–9?

Resources

Kendall Vanderslice, *We Will Feast: Rethinking Dinner, Worship, and the Community of God* (Grand Rapids: Eerdmans, 2019).

Lenny Duncan, *Dear Church: A Love Letter from a Black Preacher to the Whitest Denomination in the US* (Minneapolis: Fortress Press, 2019).

Jonathan Brooks, *Church Forsaken: Practicing Presence in Neglected Neighborhoods* (Downers Grove, IL: InterVarsity Press, 2018).

Tim Shapiro and Kara Faris, *Divergent Church: The Bright Promise of Alternative Faith Communities* (Nashville: Abingdon, 2017).

Robyn Henderson Espinoza, *Activist Theology* (Minneapolis: Fortress Press, 2019).

Stuart Murray, *Post-Christendom: Church and Mission in a Strange New World*, 2nd ed. (Eugene, OR: Cascade, 2018).

Safwat Marzouk, *Intercultural Church: A Biblical Vision for an Age of Migration* (Minneapolis: Fortress Press, 2019).

8

Invitation

The best way to not feel hopeless is to get up and do something.
Don't wait for good things to happen to you.
If you go out and make some good things happen,
you will fill the world with hope,
you will fill yourself with hope.

—Barack Obama

Final chapter . . . well, sort of! In a lot of ways, it's less a final chapter and more a dénouement. As you may know, *dénouement* is a French word that literally means "the action of untying." The term is most often used in literature, theatre, and film to capture the notion of an "end" that is simultaneously a "new beginning." Picture the conclusion of a fairy tale, which ends with the most famous line in literature, ". . . and they lived happily ever after!"

We all know enough about life to understand that "living happily ever after" is a whole new story. It's a dénouement. It's the end of a story that is a whole new story. So it is with this book. This short chapter invites a whole new story of discovery for you and your community(ies).

What's more, this era of accelerating change is shaping up to be a dénouement for the entire globe and all life that calls the earth its home! Truly, the end of this book is a new beginning. It presents to you and the group(s) you influence a glorious dare to follow the Spirit of God into joining with the rest of God's diverse creation in the dance of **anticipating** some of the changes that are likely to come our way; to **reflect** on God's shalomic dream for all of creation; and then to join with others in **innovating** new ways of doing life, deepening community, living faithfully present, and even innovating as Christ's church.

The fact that you've stuck with us throughout this journey suggests that you already have a sense, deep in your being, that even more significant change is likely on the horizon. We have only scratched the surface of coming changes in this volume. Some of these coming changes are already invoking fear, despair, and a myriad of other feelings for many people all over the world, from people in your neighborhood, and at times—if you are honest—in your own heart. Us too!

Yet even though the temptation to operate from a place of fear rears its ugly head from time to time, you choose love—love which casts out fear.[1] You choose God's sacrificial love over fear.[2] You don't grieve as the world does,[3] for you are a prisoner of hope.[4] The resurrection of Christ is

---

1.   1 John 4:7–18.

2.   Dan White Jr., *Love Over Fear: Facing Monsters, Befriending Enemies, and Healing Our Polarized World* (Chicago: Moody Press, 2019).

3.   1 Thessalonians 4:13–18.

4.   Judith Hertog, "Prisoner of Hope: Cornel West's Quest for Justice," *The Sun*, September 2018, https://tinyurl.com/uwu8zny.

not simply a means for escaping this world, nor is it some kind of delusional fantasy that it'll all work out for you and the ones you love. Rather, resurrection hope looks death in the eye and says, "You're not the boss of me!" It looks grief and suffering in the eye and does not turn away. Resurrection hope plays a cosmic, though at times painfully real, game of chicken with evil, and evil always flinches.

Christ's resurrection is the ground of hope for your belief that what might appear to be inevitable is really a Holy Spirit invitation to join God in the remaking of all creation. This is redemption. This is salvation. You have known redemption; you have known salvation. And the good news is that God is making all things new. These crises are our chance! This is your chance! What the world sees as impending doom you see as a shalomic design opportunity.

As you know, the real work of change-making does not reside with the researchers, writers, theoreticians, or politicians, but with real people like us, like you, and the group(s) with whom you do life—real people, doing life in real communities, for the sake of thriving within and beyond their real neighborhoods. As the great cultural anthropologist Margaret Mead is often quoted as saying, "Never underestimate the power of a small group of committed people to change the world. In fact, it is the only thing that ever has." The 2020s Foresight revolution starts with you and your group.

Just before Jesus's ascension, he commissioned a small group of people, saying, "As you go about your everyday lives, form followers in my Way, teaching them to live out of an imagination for the shalom of God, marking them with the unity of diversity that is the triune life of God, and daring them to live lives of faithful presence.

Remember, you are not alone. For I am with you making all things new."[5]

Jesus's commissioning of his disciples extends to us as well. We are all invited to join God and all of creation in God's shalomic plan to make all things new:

> Behold, I am doing a new thing;
> Now it springs forth, do you not perceive it?
> I will make a way in the wilderness and rivers in the desert.[6]

As this book comes to a close, we would like to offer you a benediction, a sending, a dénouement. As you are just a few paragraphs away from setting down this book, we invite you onto the dance floor. The rhythm of the music is playing God's shalomic three-step, a tune that you've heard throughout this book. **Anticipating . . . Reflecting . . . Innovating**—steps you will repeat often.

You Are Being Invited to Dance

The music is beautiful. The music simultaneously resonates with every innovative tune played throughout history, reverberating through the universe and within your own body, while beating with the freshness and tensions of the multitudinous accelerating changes charging toward you and yours. The music is edgy, a little scary, and divinely familiar. It calls to you. Its rhythm's pulse beats like the throbbing of your heart. It woos you to life; it might, in fact, be life.

The dance floor is your place. Right where you are. Your

---

5. Matthew 28:19–20, Dwight's paraphrase.
6. Isaiah 43:19 (ESV). The "I" in this text is not Isaiah but God. God is doing a new thing!

neighborhood! Here and now! The dance floor is almost always a dare. Will you give yourself over to that which is wooing you toward life and innovation, or will you self-consciously hold back for fear of what others might think?

There is no room on this dance floor for choreographed perfection. Rather, God's shalomic rhythm calls for shalomic freestyle. You must innovate, and this can feel risky . . . because it is risky. You will put yourself out there, maybe like Noah building an ark, maybe like Tabitha making clothing for the "widows" of Joppa, maybe like many of the people in the stories told throughout this book. What is your dance floor inviting?

Dancing is the integration of "leading" and "following" within a particular context. That is what you are embarking on. The world tells people to seize the day, to take the lead, to force their dance steps on those with less power, privilege, or influence. But the Gospels reframe the dance.

Transformative power is in following—following God, being changed by others, and learning from your context. The apostle Paul called this "keeping in step with the Spirit."[7] Most of the coming crises our world is facing are the unintended consequences of powerful people asserting the lead.

Seizing the lead roles is not the way forward in an era of accelerating change. Following the Jesus Way is the only way forward. Listening, feeling, and courageously moving to the rhythm of God's shalomic music. Who is your partner in this dance? Who are you? Honestly, these may be the most profound questions you explore throughout this whole book.

While Western culture wants you to think of yourself as a

---

7. Galatians 5:16–26.

rugged individual, that is not who you really are . . . but you have always known that there is more to your self-identity. Yes, you are absolutely unique! There is no one exactly like you; yet your desires reflect the desires of nearly every person on the globe. Yes, you are absolutely unique, and you are part of a larger body of people. Your loving dance partner is a complex mystery of the Holy Trinity; together you are dancing with God, with others, and with the land you inhabit.

How will you dance with your partner(s)? Who will lead? Please, for the sake of your own joy and maybe for your great-grandchildren, open yourself to being led. Resist the Christendom assumption to claim leadership. Don't take charge. Don't cast a big vision for your alternative future. Rather, listen. Love. Attend. Respond. And join. Learn the way of whole-life followership. Let God, diverse others, and your place guide you into the vital dance of **anticipating**, **reflecting**, and **innovating**.

By now we hope you feel the rhythm of those three dance steps. As this book closes, we dare you to engage in no-holds-barred forecasting. We encourage you to peer into the deep, especially those things that most fill you or your group with fear, and not turn away. Dare to anticipate the wide array of changes that are coming your way. Look those things square in the eye. What might be the worst coming your way? What might those changes invite? What is possible? What is probable? We bless you to take it all in.

Reflect on the hope-filled narrative of Holy Scripture. As you do, you will see that God is not thwarted by evil. Rather, God turns evil on its head, extracting divine beauty from ugliness; it's what God does!

We encourage you and your group to reflect on God's great love for all creation, to reflect on the extent to which

God continues to woo all that is into reconciled relationship. The dance step of reflection is a sincere practice of communal discernment. Together with fellow followers of the Jesus way, discern your way forward; as a local collective, seek to follow the Lord Jesus Christ into rendering more visible the redemptive dream of God.

Reflecting on God's shalom will naturally lead you and your group to action. We bless you into this innovative dance step. Innovation certainly requires courage. But when you think about what might happen if you choose not to act, that's even scarier. Choosing not to innovate is to enthrone the status quo.

And so—like Christ—for the joy set before you, you and your group will innovate. Don't worry if not everyone understands why you're doing what you're doing. Some other Christians may call you a heretic or tell you that you've lost your way. Those who have conflated the American dream with God's shalomic dream may despise you and seek your demise, and those who celebrate nationalism more than the reign of God may see you as a threat.

Innovation is no small risk. And there is no guarantee of success. You might give your life to being faithfully present to the environment, and the polar ice caps still melt. Innovation through faithful presence is not about results; it's about discovering the love of God through loving your neighbors as you love yourself. Do you need to win, or are you wooed to love as Christ loves?

We are confident that you sense the call to love as Christ loves. We bless you! You were born for a time such as this. You and your group are needed . . . here and now!

Receive the words from a tribute offered in memory of Oscar Romero, Archbishop of San Salvador, as your invitation to the vital forecasting dance.

A Future Not Our Own

It helps now and then to step back and take a long view. The Kingdom is not only beyond our efforts; it is beyond our vision.

We accomplish in our lifetime only a fraction of the magnificent enterprise that is God's work.

Nothing we do is complete, which is another way of saying that the kingdom always lies beyond us.

No statement says all that could be said.

No prayer fully expresses our faith.

No confession brings perfection.

No pastoral visit brings wholeness.

No program accomplishes the Church's mission.

No set of goals and objectives include everything.

This is what we are about. We plant the seeds that one day will grow.

We water the seeds already planted knowing that they hold future promise.

We lay foundations that will need further development.

We provide yeast that produces effects far beyond our capabilities.

We cannot do everything, and there is a sense of liberation in realizing this.

This enables us to do something, and to do it very well.

It may be incomplete, but it is a beginning, a step along the way, an opportunity for the Lord's grace to enter and do the rest.

We may never see the end results, but that is the difference between the master builder and the worker.

We are workers, not master builders, ministers, not messiahs. We are prophets of a future not our own.[8]

Prayer

Commissioning God,

Remind us that we are ministers, not Messiahs. We are workers, not master builders. We are innovators, not the Creator or the Redeemer. By your Spirit, enable us to tap into our resurrection hope, which compels us to look into the reality of the accelerating changes that are racing toward us, yet not turn away. May we not live in denial, but with Christ-like hope; may we lean in. As we lean in, we ask for shalomic imaginations—not even fully knowing what that means—to innovate for our best lives, to innovate for all who come after us, and to innovate as responsible stewards of the earth you entrusted to us, and of which we are a part. Thank you that you are with us; we are not alone. May this vital dance live on in us. Amen.

---

8. A prayer composed by Bishop Ken Untener of Saginaw, Michigan, and offered as a tribute to Oscar A. Romero (1917–1980), Archbishop of San Salvador, in El Salvador, who was assassinated on March 24, 1980, while celebrating Mass in a small chapel in the cancer hospital where he lived. This prayer was drafted as a homily by Cardinal John Dearden in November 1979 for a celebration of departed priests.

For Group Discussion

1. So you're at the end of this book, which is also the beginning of the rest of your life. What are your next steps toward meaningful anticipation of the changes that will likely impact you and your place in this era of accelerating changes?

2. As you reflect on the character of God and God's dream for creation, how might these coming changes serve as a shalomic design opportunity to discover the Jesus Way?

3. Given who you are, where you are, and who you're there with, what might be yours to do? You can't do everything, but this means you can do something. So, what will it be?

4. Of all the incoming waves of change, where do you sense God's innovation? In your personal life and closest relationships? With those you work with in your organization? Within the ecosystem of relationships in your neighborhood?

Resources

Elaine Scarry, *On Beauty and Being Just* (Princeton: Princeton University Press, 2013).

James Davison Hunter, *To Change the World: The Irony, Tragedy, and Possibility of Christianity in the Late Modern World* (Oxford: Oxford University Press, 2010).

Rosaria Champagne Butterfield, *The Gospel Comes with a House Key: Practicing Radically Ordinary Hospitality in Our Post-Christian World* (Wheaton, IL: Crossway, 2018).